The Magical Friends
in the
Land Of Variance

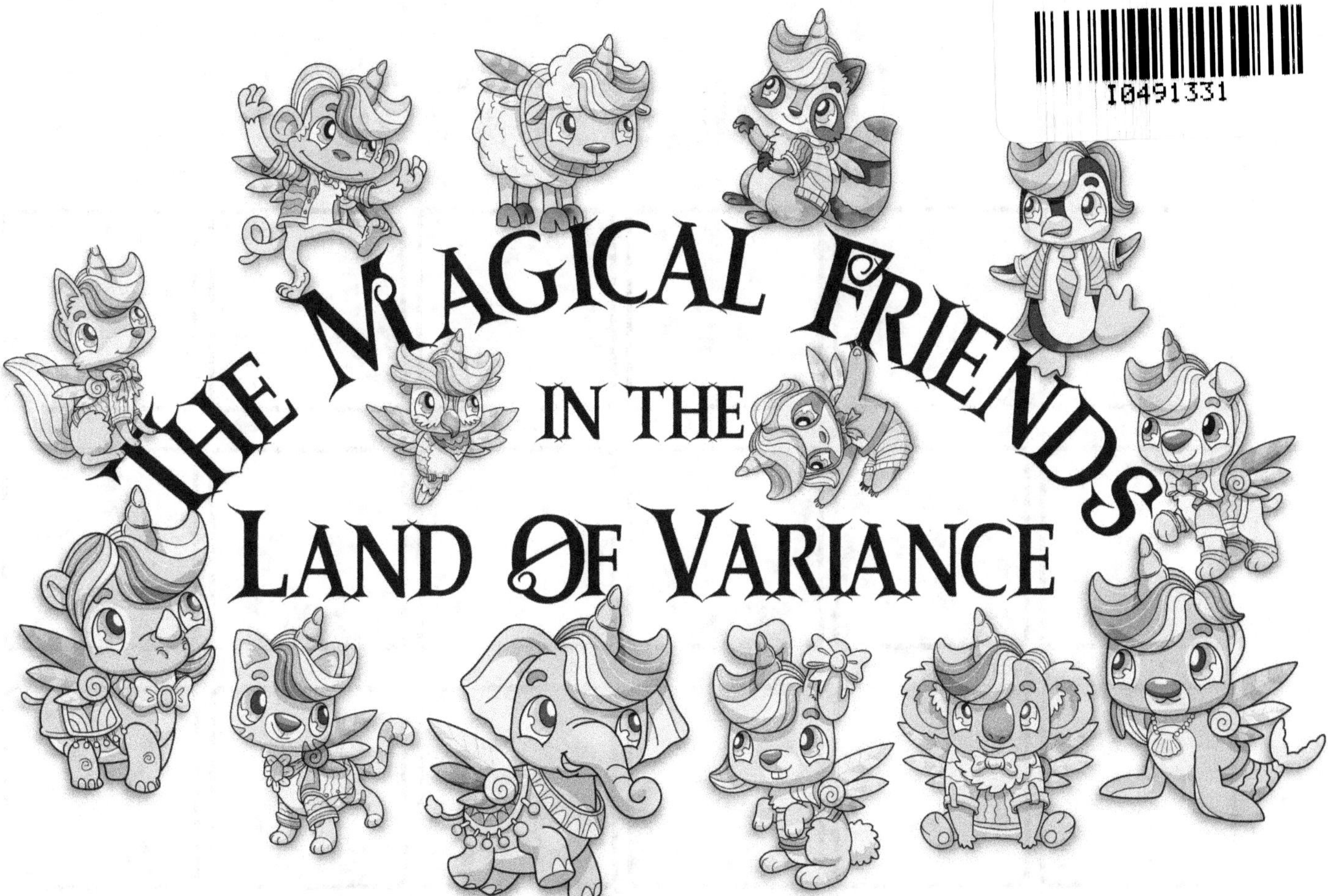

Coloring and Activity Book

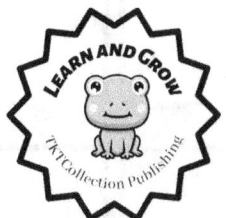

THIS BOOK IS DEDICATED TO:

THE WORLD OF WARCRAFT GUILD
VARIANCE.
AND THE MEMBERS THESE CHARACTERS ARE NAMED IN HONOR OF.
THANK YOU FOR YOUR ACCEPTANCE, PATIENCE, KNOWLEDGE AND MOSTLY IMPORTANTLY
FRIENDSHIP.

LOVE, KRYSNYA!

For permissions requests or inquiries, please contact:
TKTCollectionPublishing.com

Color Test Page

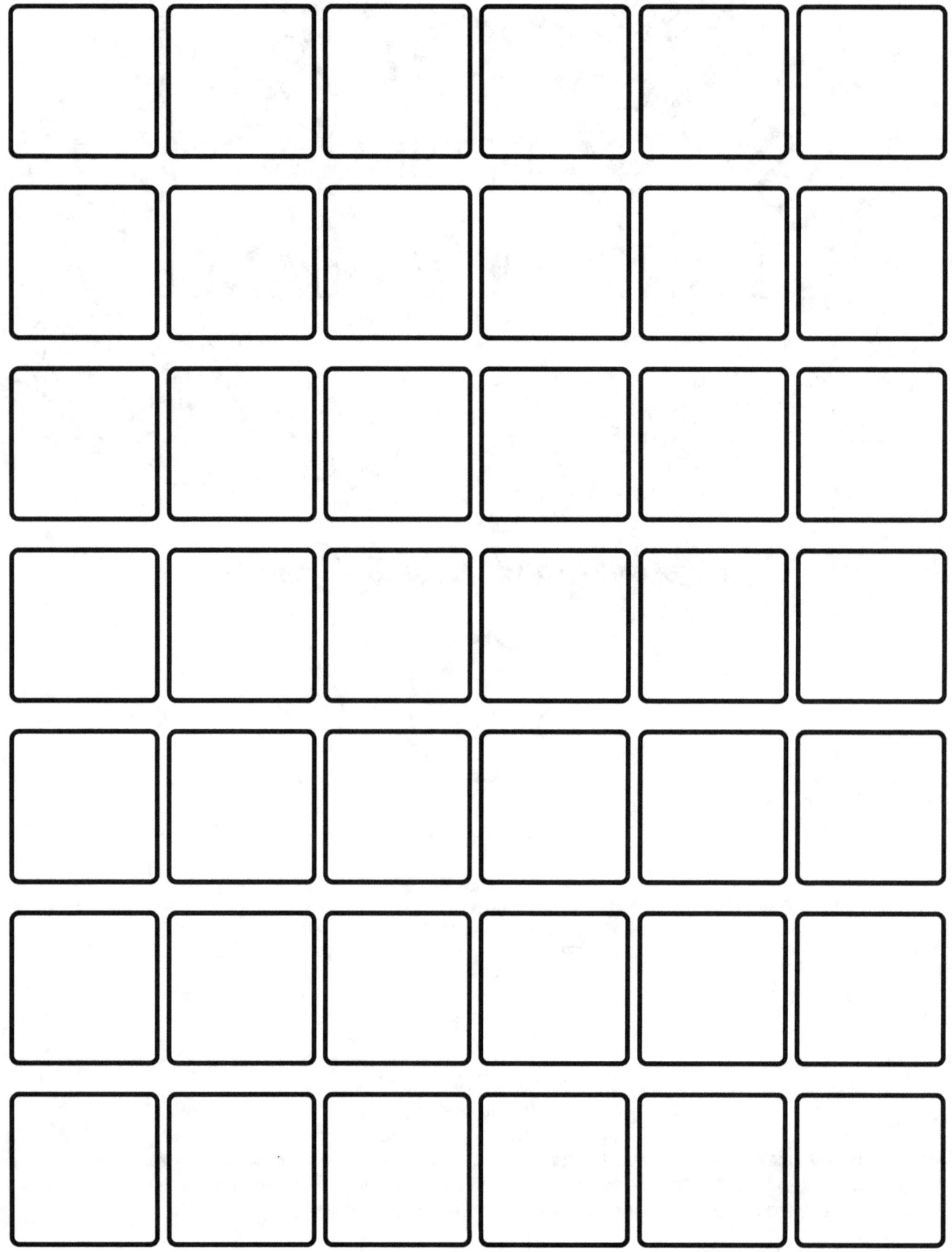

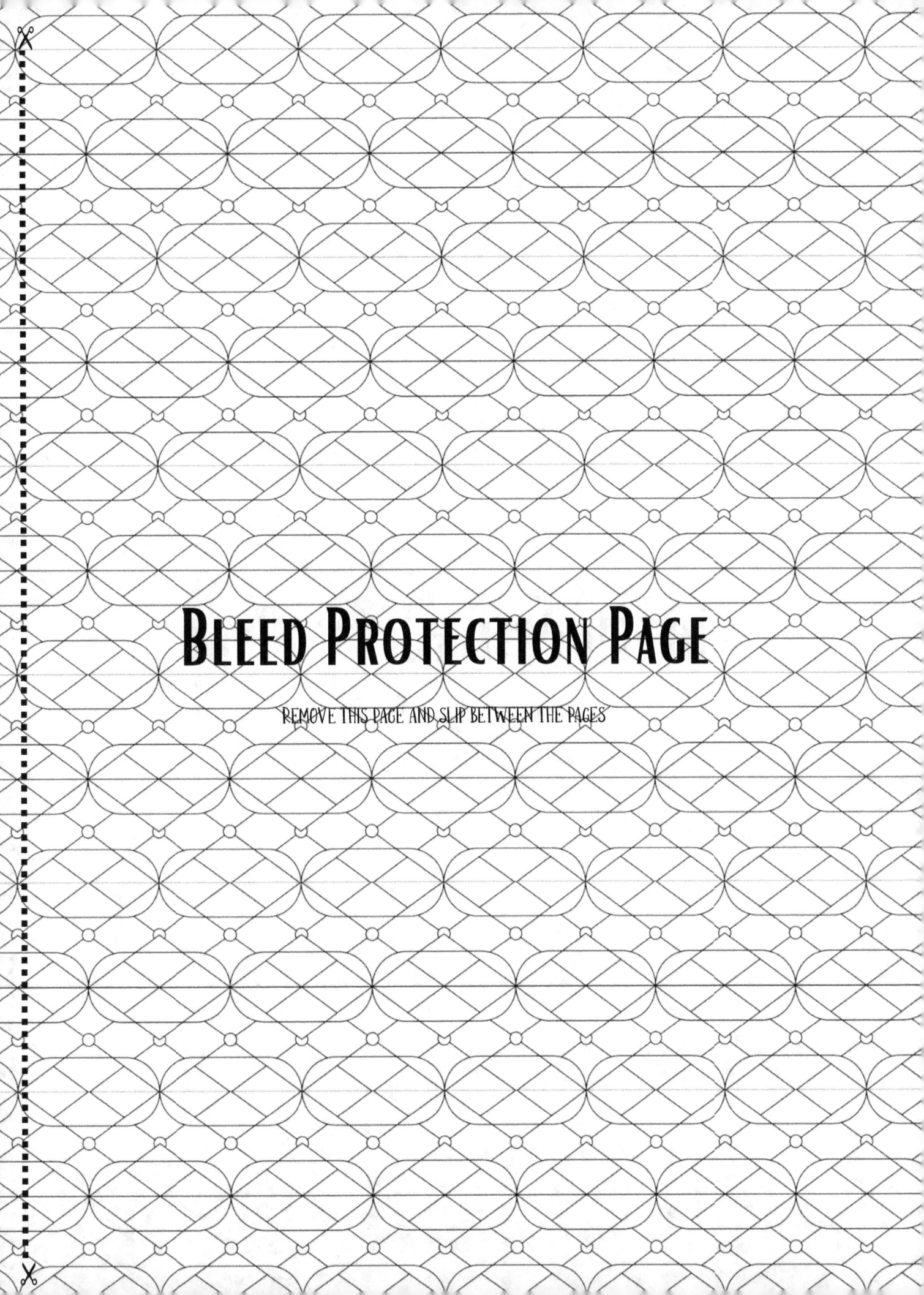

BLEED PROTECTION PAGE

REMOVE THIS PAGE AND SLIP BETWEEN THE PAGES

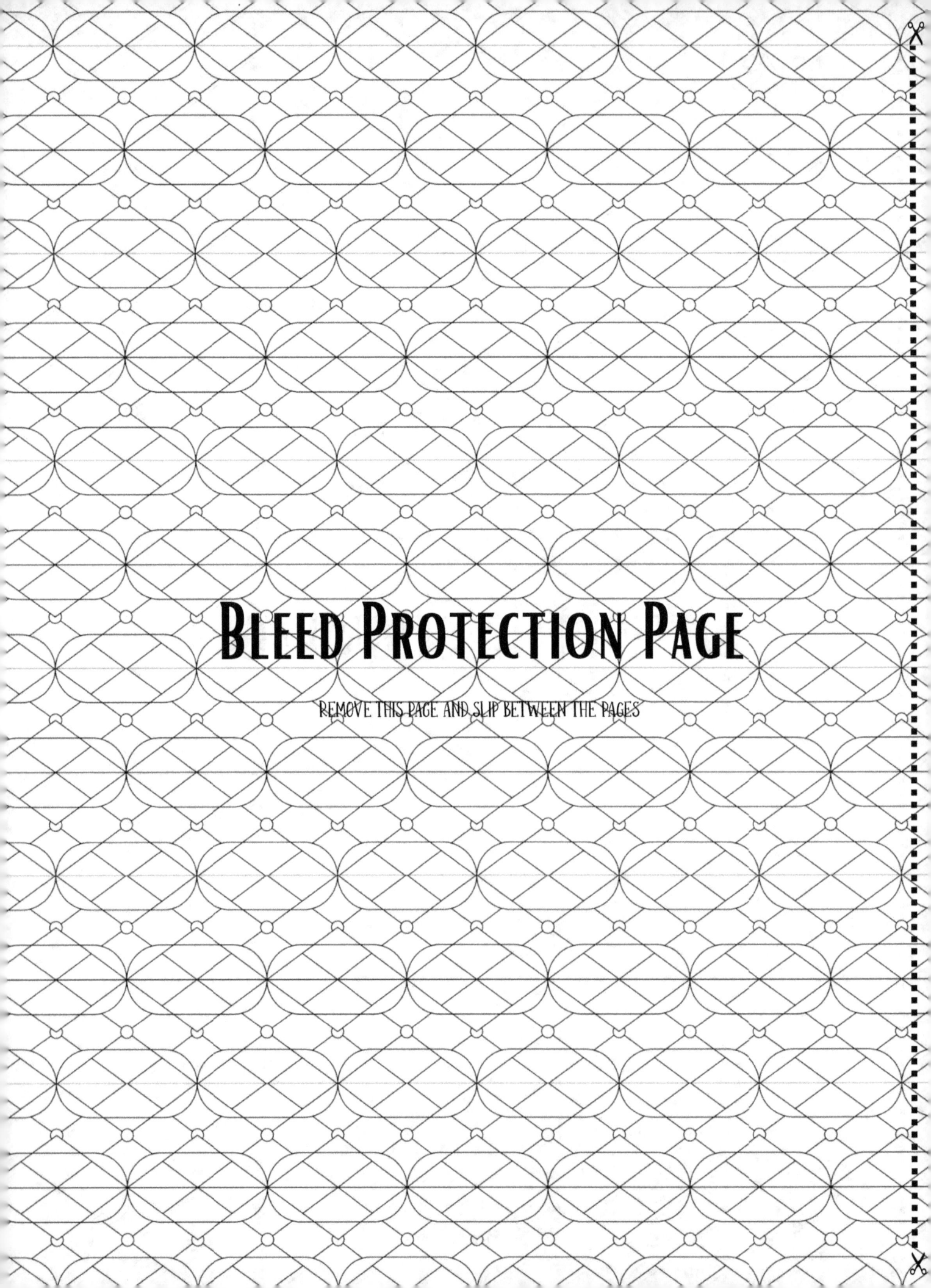

Bleed Protection Page

REMOVE THIS PAGE AND SLIP BETWEEN THE PAGES

MORVAS
THE ENERGETIC SQUIRREL

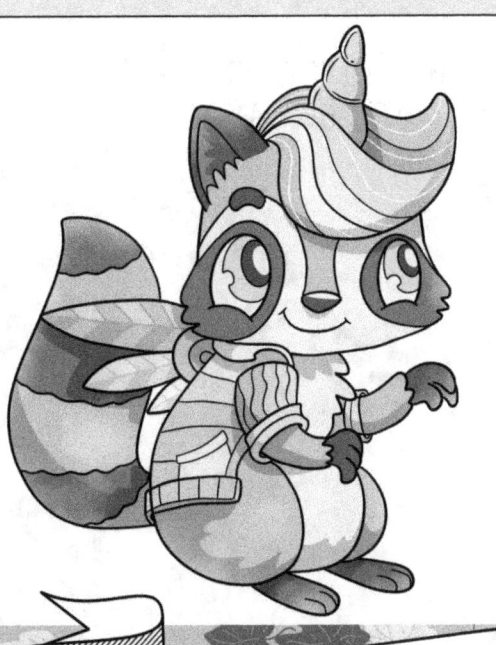

TRAITS: ENERGETIC, MISCHIEVOUS, QUICK-WITTED.

LIKES: RACING THROUGH TREETOPS, GATHERING SHINY OBJECTS, SURPRISING FRIENDS.

DISLIKES: BEING STILL, LOSING RACES, BEING TOLD TO SLOW DOWN.

FUN FACT: MORVAS CAN CRACK THE TOUGHEST NUT IN VARIANCE WITH A SINGLE ACORN!

MORVAS AND THE NUTTY CHALLENGE

IN THE VIBRANT LAND OF VARIANCE, MORVAS THE ENERGETIC SQUIRREL WAS RENOWNED FOR HIS AGILITY. ONE SUNNY DAY, A NUT-GATHERING RACE WAS ANNOUNCED, AND MORVAS WAS DETERMINED TO PROVE HIS SKILLS. THE RACE LED THROUGH A WHIMSICAL OBSTACLE COURSE FILLED WITH SWINGING VINES, WOBBLING BRIDGES, AND TUNNELS OF LEAVES. MORVAS LEAPED, DASHED, AND LAUGHED HIS WAY THROUGH, DISPLAYING INCREDIBLE ACROBATICS. BUT THE FINAL CHALLENGE WAS A TOWERING TREE WITH THE MOST DELICIOUS NUTS AT ITS TOP. WITH BOUNDLESS DETERMINATION, MORVAS CONQUERED THE TREE, CLAIMING VICTORY AND A BASKET OF NUTS FOR HIS FRIENDS.

Nutty Obstacle Course

Join Morvas on his nutty adventure!

Draw Morvas in the obstacle course, as he collects nuts 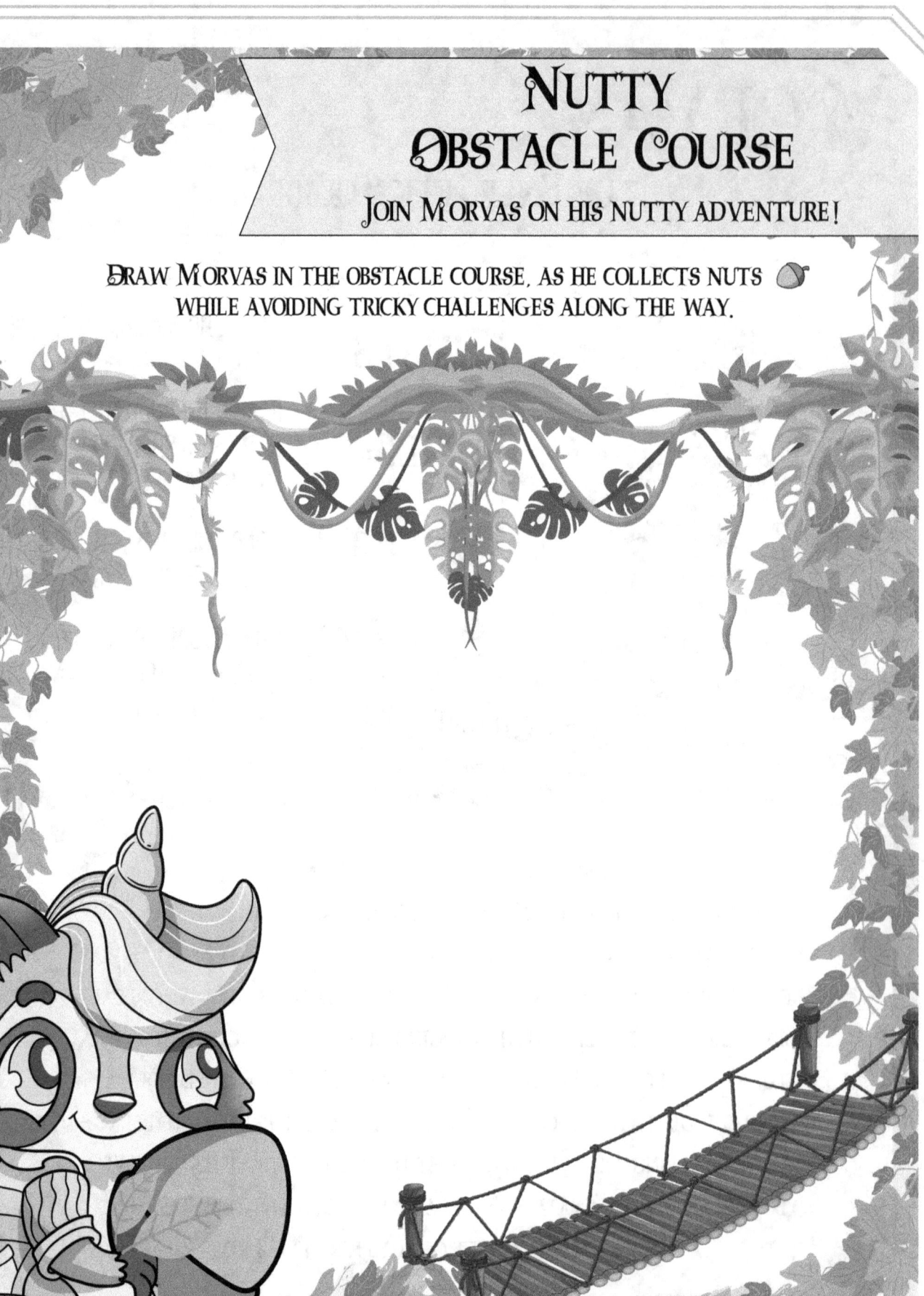 while avoiding tricky challenges along the way.

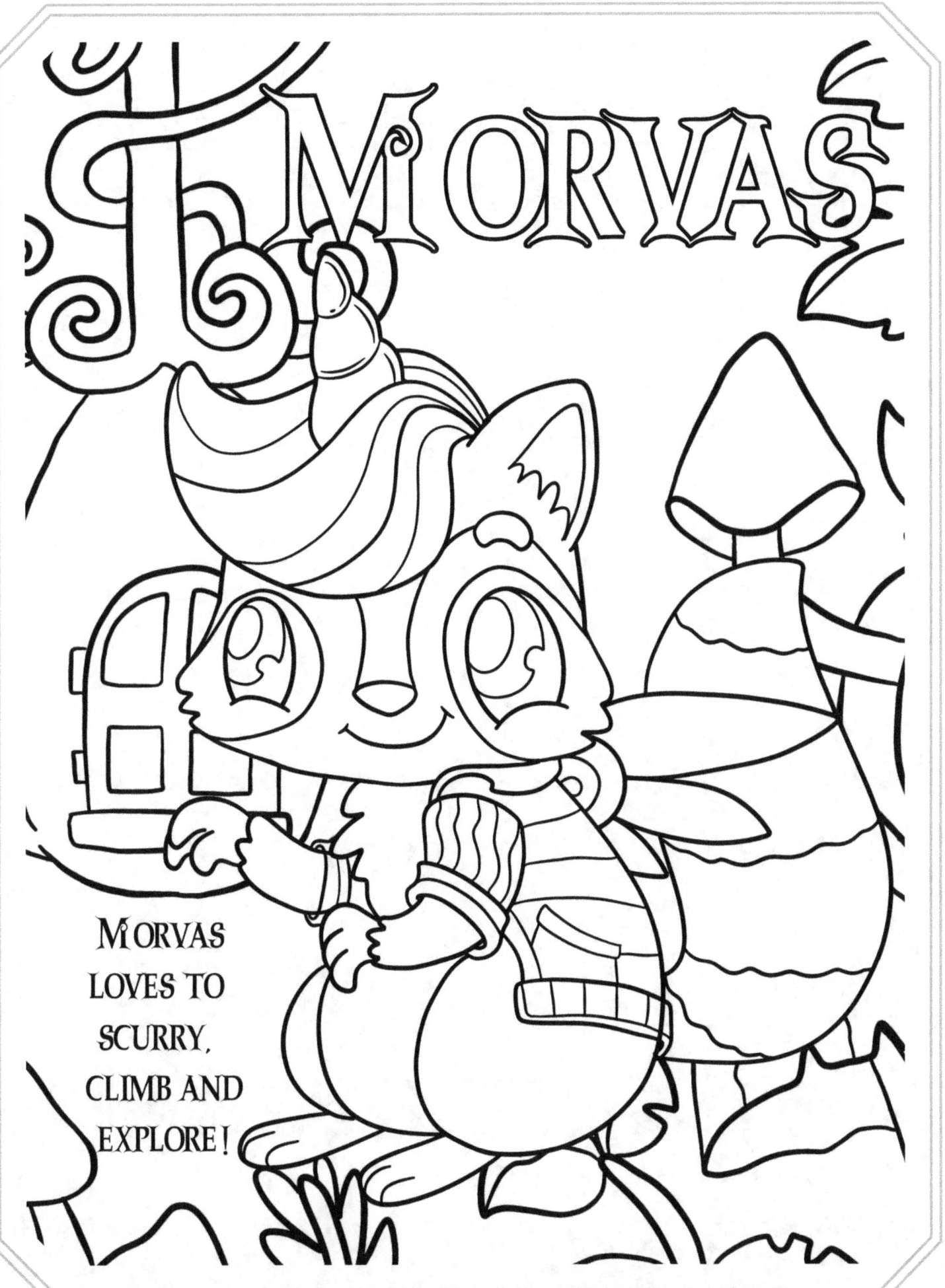

MORVAS

MORVAS LOVES TO SCURRY, CLIMB AND EXPLORE!

Magical Friends in Land of Variance

Completed By:

Date:

WATTS

THE WISE ELEPHANT

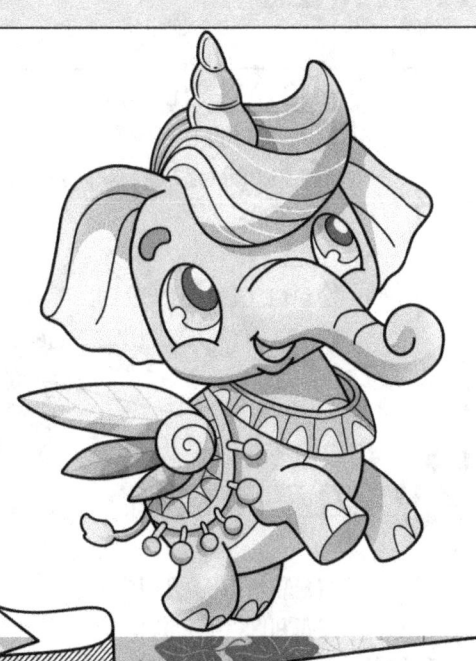

TRAITS: WISE, PATIENT, GENTLE.

LIKES: SOLVING RIDDLES, LISTENING TO STORIES, HELPING OTHERS.

DISLIKES: RUSHING, LOUD NOISES, UNNECESSARY ARGUMENTS.

FUN FACT: WATTS HAS AN INCREDIBLE MEMORY AND NEVER FORGETS A FRIEND'S BIRTHDAY!

WATTS AND THE ENCHANTED PUZZLE

IN THE HEART OF VARIANCE, WHERE WISDOM BLOSSOMED LIKE FLOWERS, LIVED WATTS THE WISE ELEPHANT. ONE DAY, A PECULIAR PUZZLE ARRIVED, ITS PIECES SCATTERED THROUGHOUT THE LAND. WATTS, KNOWN FOR HIS INTELLECT, TOOK ON THE CHALLENGE. AS HE GATHERED PIECES, HE UNCOVERED THAT EACH HELD A FRAGMENT OF A MAGICAL MAP. ASSEMBLING THE PUZZLE, AN ANCIENT PATH REVEALED ITSELF, LEADING TO THE HIDDEN GARDEN OF UNITY. THERE, WATTS DISCOVERED A SPARKLING FOUNTAIN, ITS WATERS RADIATING HARMONY. WATTS KNEW THAT UNITY WAS THE KEY TO VARIANCE'S STRENGTH, AND HE VOWED TO SHARE THIS REVELATION WITH HIS FRIENDS.

ACTIVITY: PUZZLE MAP

CREATE YOUR OWN!

Begin your exciting journey by imagining you're in Variance, following the path that Watts took to discover the Garden of Unity.

ITEMS NEEDED:
- BLANK PAPER
- MARKERS OR COLORED PENCILS
- SCISSORS
- GLUE OR TAPE
- SMALL CONTAINER OR ENVELOPE (FOR PUZZLE PIECES)

INSTRUCTIONS

1 CREATE A MAP:

- ON A BLANK PIECE OF PAPER, DRAW A MAP THAT SHOWS THE LANDMARKS AND PATH TO THE GARDEN OF UNITY.
- USE YOUR IMAGINATION TO MAKE IT EXCITING AND INTRIGUING.
- USE MARKERS OR COLORED PENCILS TO COLOR EACH PUZZLE PIECE.

2 PUZZLE PIECES:

- DIVIDE YOUR MAP INTO PUZZLE PIECES.
- DRAW LINES ACROSS THE PAPER TO CREATE PUZZLE-SHAPED SECTIONS.
- THESE PIECES WILL REPRESENT THE DIFFERENT PARTS OF YOUR MAP.

3 CUT AND ORGANIZE:

- CAREFULLY CUT ALONG THE LINES YOU'VE DRAWN TO CREATE THE INDIVIDUAL PUZZLE PIECES.
- ONCE CUT, MAKE SURE TO KEEP THE PIECES IN ORDER.

SMALL CONTAINER OR ENVELOPE
KEEP YOUR PUZZLE SAFE AND ORGANIZED, IN A SMALL CONTAINER OR ENVELOPE.

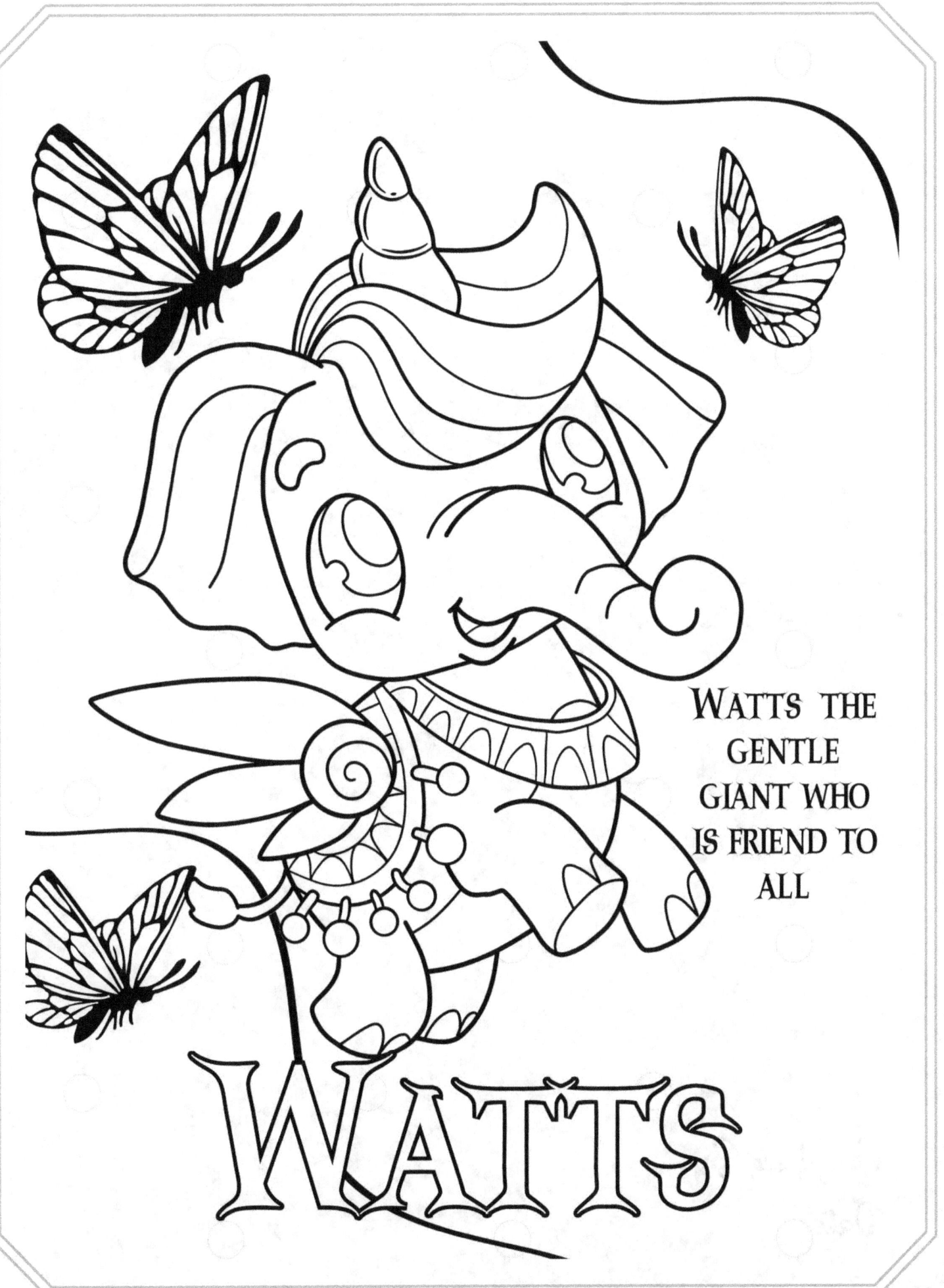

WATTS THE
GENTLE
GIANT WHO
IS FRIEND TO
ALL

WATTS

Completed By:

Date:

BRAGO
THE MISCHIEVOUS MONKEY

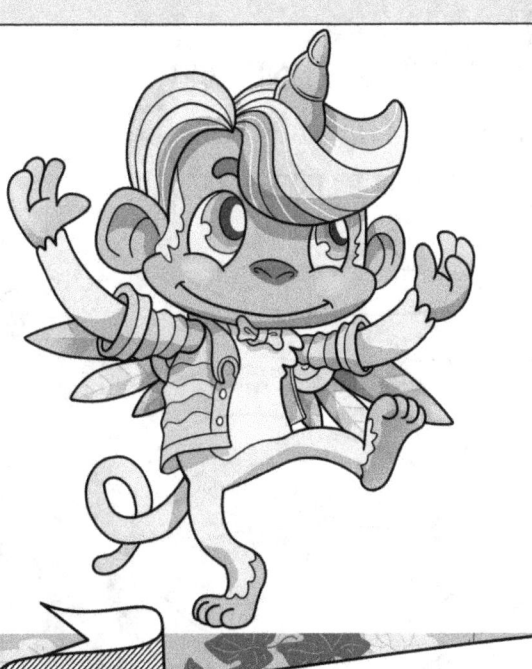

TRAITS: MISCHIEVOUS, CLEVER, AGILE.

LIKES: SWINGING THROUGH TREES, PLAYING PRANKS, FINDING HIDDEN SNACKS.

DISLIKES: BORING ROUTINES, BEING SCOLDED, RAINY DAYS.

FUN FACT: BRAGO'S TAIL CAN MIMIC THE SOUND OF A VARIANCE WATERFALL!

BRAGO'S MYSTERIOUS MAP

IN THE ENCHANTING LAND OF VARIANCE, BRAGO THE INQUISITIVE MONKEY HAD AN INSATIABLE THIRST FOR ADVENTURE. ONE SUN-DRENCHED MORNING, A SHIMMERING MAP APPEARED AT HIS DOORSTEP, ITS ORIGIN UNKNOWN. BRAGO'S CURIOSITY IGNITED, AND HE SET OFF TO UNCOVER THE MAP'S SECRETS. THROUGH LUSH JUNGLES AND SPARKLING STREAMS, BRAGO FOLLOWED THE MAP'S CRYPTIC CLUES, DISCOVERING ANCIENT LANDMARKS AND HIDDEN CAVES. AT LAST, THE TRAIL LED TO A MESMERIZING WATERFALL, ITS CASCADE CONCEALING A TREASURE CHEST. INSIDE, BRAGO FOUND NOT RICHES, BUT A MESSAGE: "THE JOURNEY WAS THE REAL TREASURE, AND FRIENDSHIP THE GREATEST REWARD."

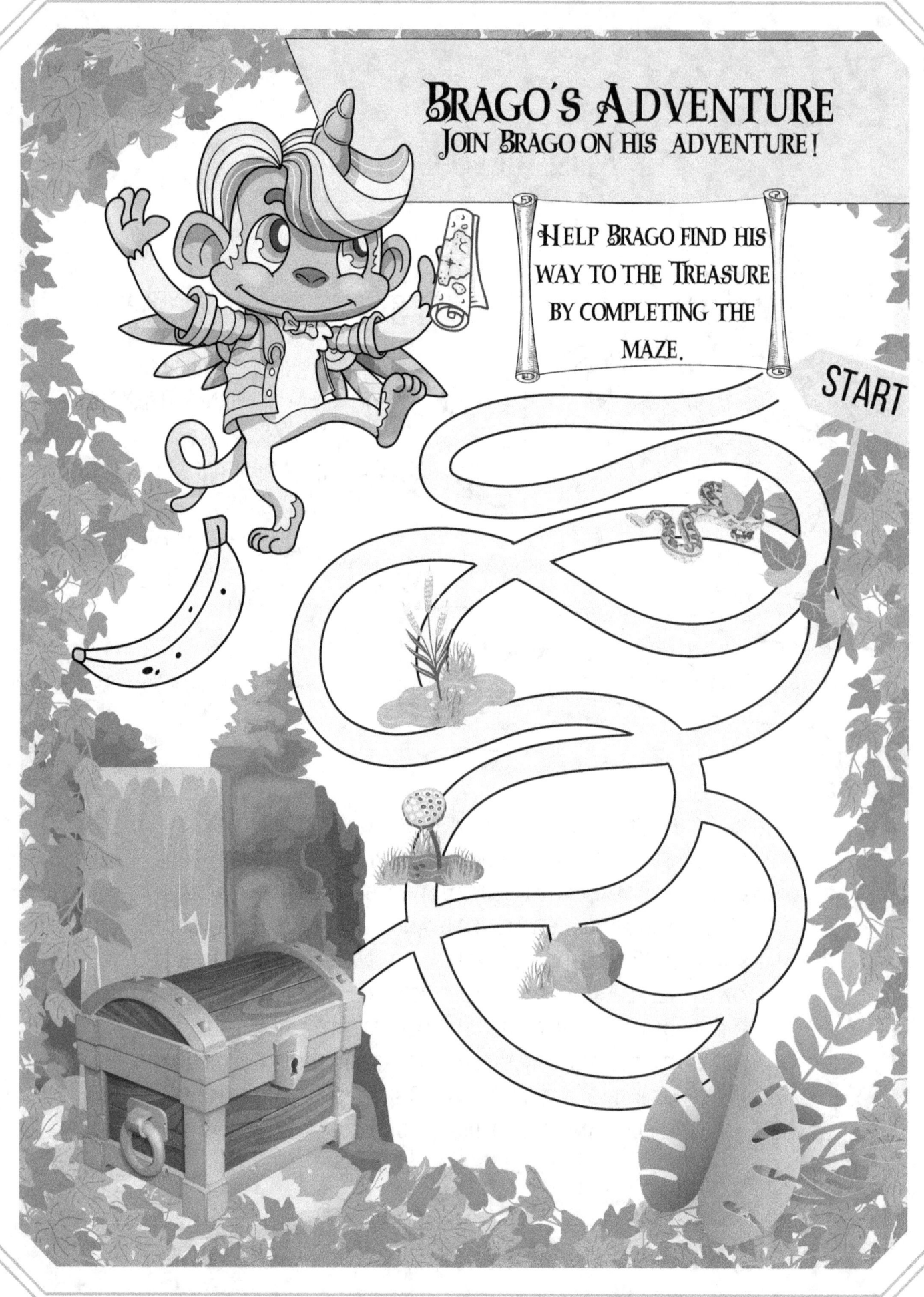

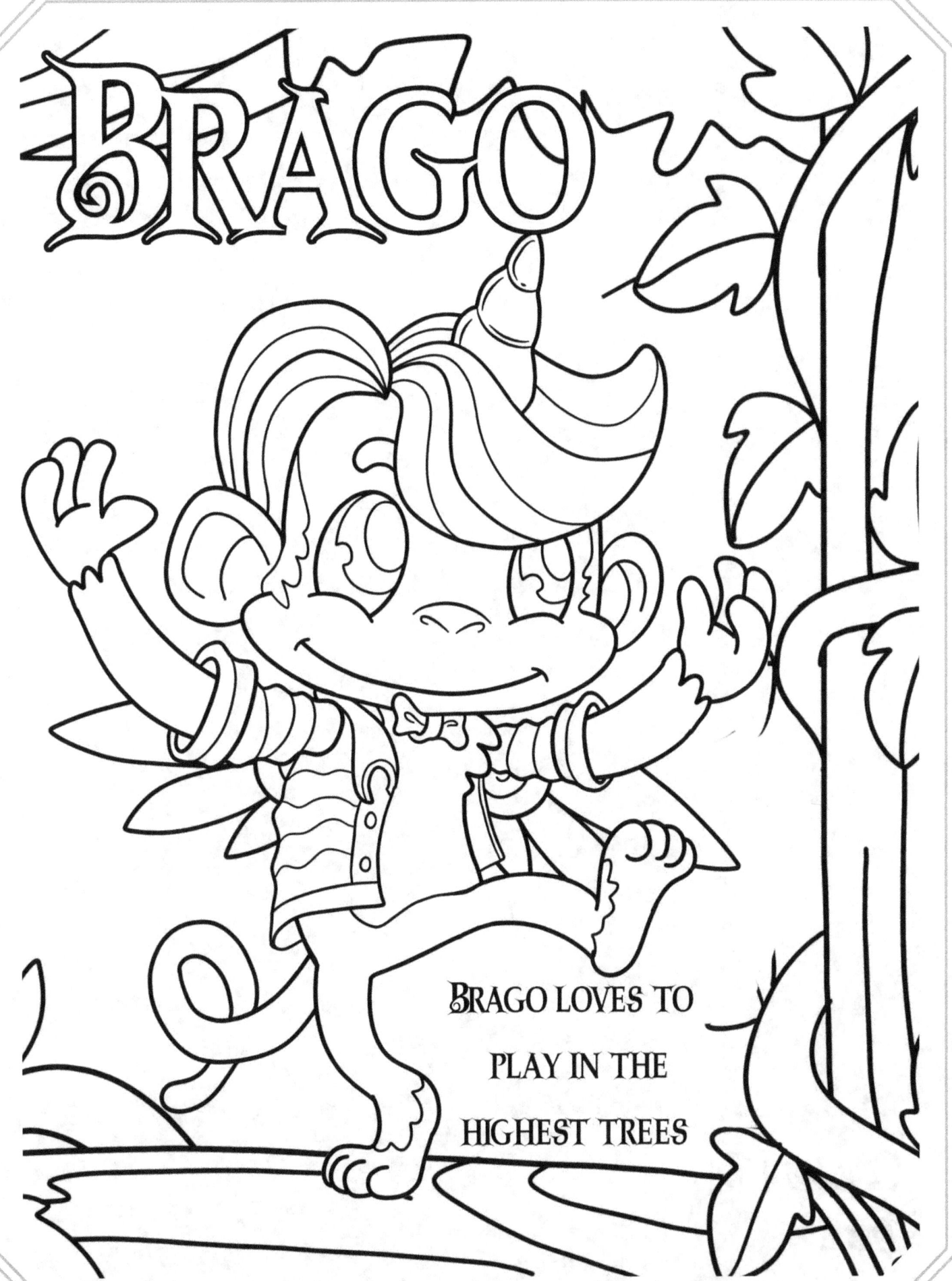

BRAGO

BRAGO LOVES TO
PLAY IN THE
HIGHEST TREES

Completed By:

Date:

DAZZY

THE GENTLE SHEEP

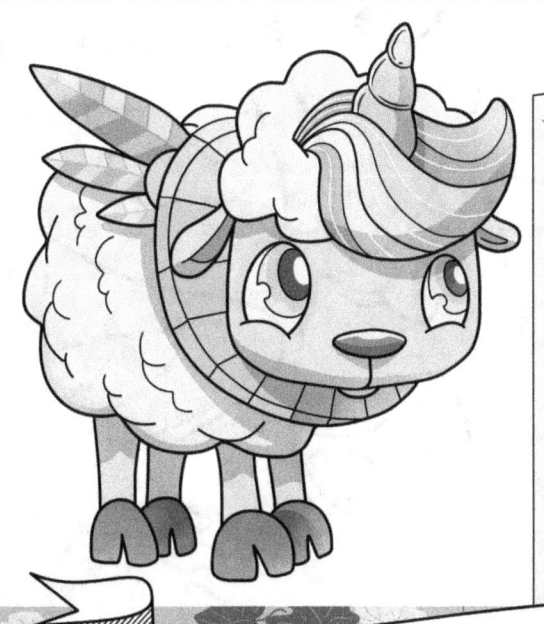

TRAITS: GENTLE, KIND-HEARTED, SHY.

LIKES: GRAZING IN MEADOWS, MAKING FRIENDS, FEELING THE GENTLE BREEZE.

DISLIKES: LOUD NOISES, SUDDEN MOVEMENTS, BEING SEPARATED FROM THE FLOCK.

FUN FACT: DAZZY'S WOOL IS THE SOFTEST AND WARMEST IN ALL OF VARIANCE!

DAZZY'S STARLIT STROLL

IN THE WHIMSICAL LAND OF VARIANCE, DAZZY THE IMAGINATIVE SHEEP OFTEN FOUND HERSELF LOST IN DAYDREAMS. ONE SUNNY AFTERNOON, DAZZY WANDERED INTO A FIELD OF VIBRANT FLOWERS. AS A GENTLE BREEZE SWIRLED AROUND HER, DAZZY CLOSED HER EYES AND MADE A WISH. TO HER AMAZEMENT, THE FLOWERS BEGAN TO SWAY IN HARMONY WITH HER THOUGHTS, CREATING A BREATHTAKING DANCE. DAZZY'S HEART FILLED WITH JOY AS SHE REALIZED THE MAGIC WITHIN HER. FROM THAT DAY ON, DAZZY'S DAYDREAMS BECAME HER WAY OF BRINGING BEAUTY AND HAPPINESS TO THE WORLD.

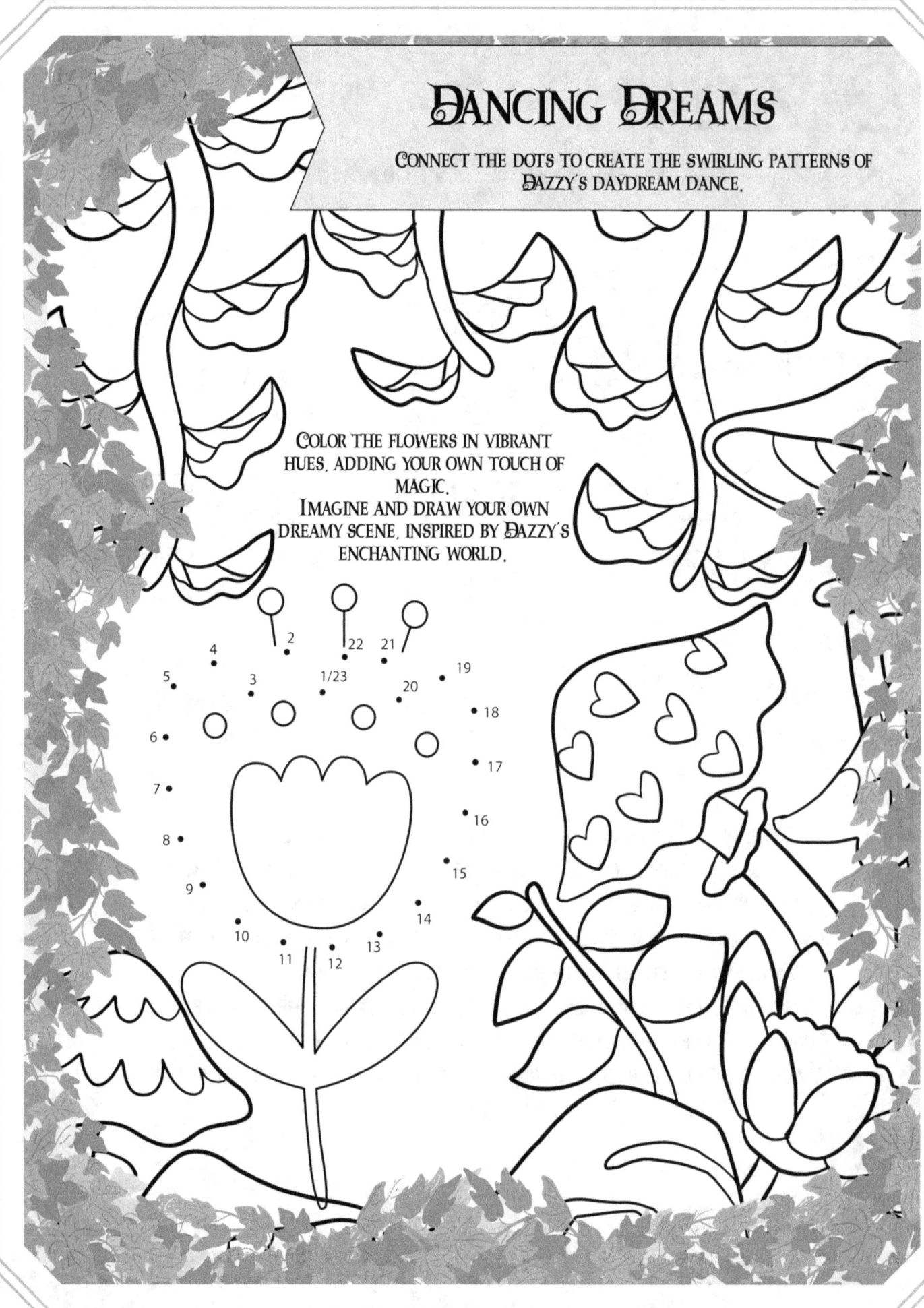

DANCING DREAMS

CONNECT THE DOTS TO CREATE THE SWIRLING PATTERNS OF
DAZZY'S DAYDREAM DANCE.

COLOR THE FLOWERS IN VIBRANT
HUES, ADDING YOUR OWN TOUCH OF
MAGIC.
IMAGINE AND DRAW YOUR OWN
DREAMY SCENE, INSPIRED BY DAZZY'S
ENCHANTING WORLD.

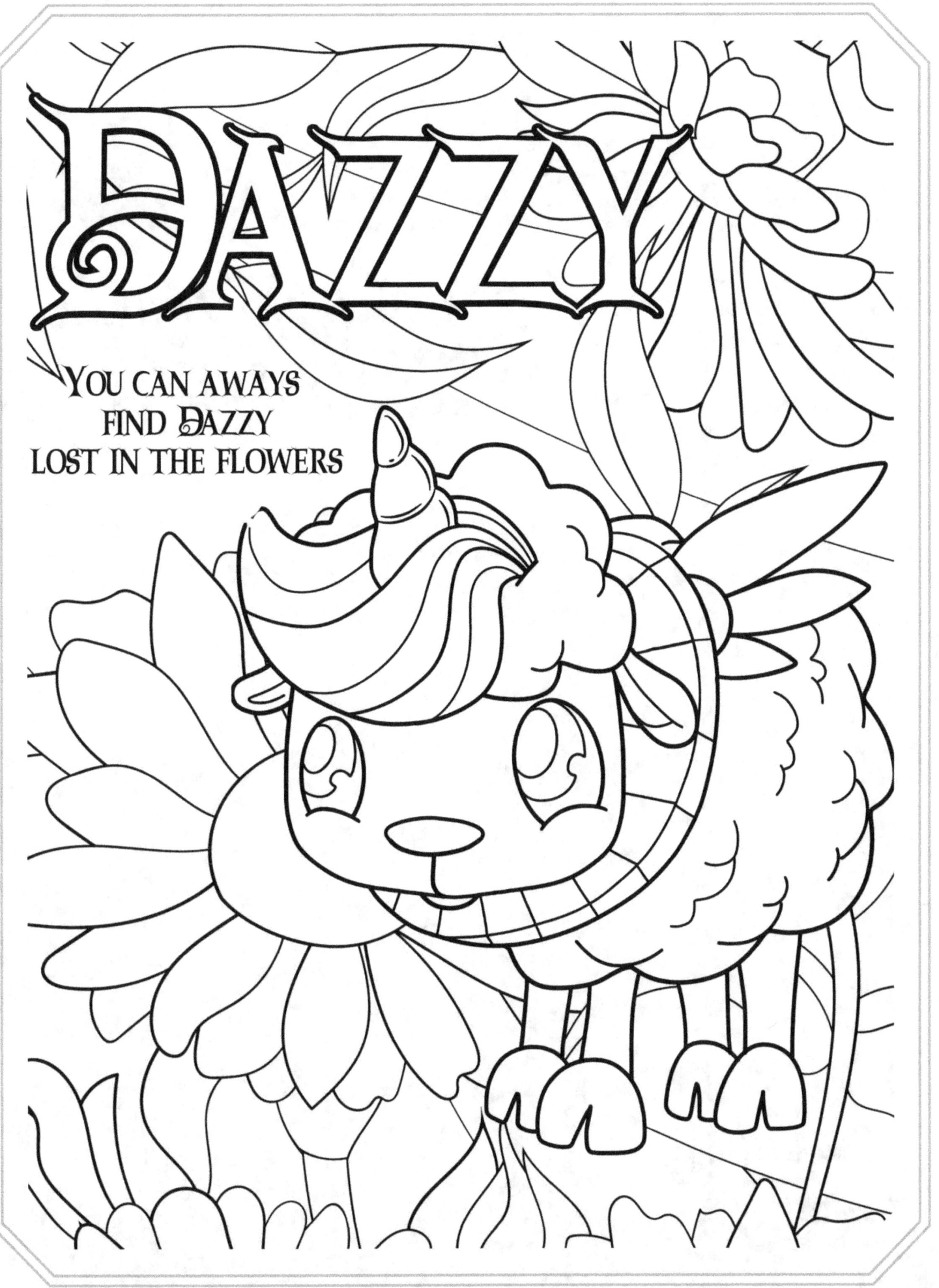

Completed By:

Date:

LUNA

THE CURIOUS CAT

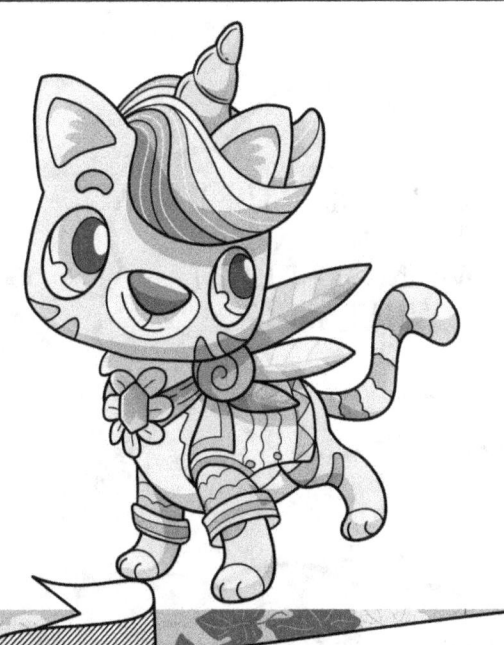

TRAITS: CURIOUS, OBSERVANT, AGILE.

LIKES: EXPLORING HIDDEN PATHS, GAZING AT STARS, FINDING NEW TREASURES.

DISLIKES: CLOSED DOORS, MISSING OUT ON ADVENTURES, RAINY DAYS.

FUN FACT: LUNA'S TAIL CAN TWITCH IN MORSE CODE!

LUNA'S NIGHT ADVENTURE

IN VARIANCE, WHERE MOONLIGHT PAINTED DREAMS, LUNA THE CURIOUS CAT EMBARKED ON A QUEST. GUIDED BY FIREFLIES, SHE MET THE ANCIENT RIDDLE OAK. "SOLVE MY RIDDLES," IT WHISPERED. LUNA'S MIND SPARKLED AS SHE UNRAVELED MYSTERIES, EARNING THE TREE'S TRUST.

A SECRET PASSAGE LED LUNA TO A CRYSTAL CHAMBER, REVEALING VARIANCE'S HISTORY. SHE EMERGED, HEART BRIMMING WITH TALES. LUNA SHARED THEM WITH FRIENDS, FIREFLIES SWIRLING AROUND, CREATING MELODIES. LUNA, GUARDIAN OF STORIES, EMBRACED THE NIGHT, HER CURIOSITY FOREVER KINDLING THE LAND'S MAGIC.

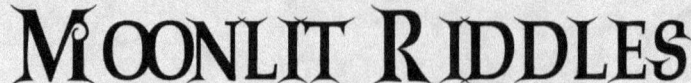

MOONLIT RIDDLES

SOLVE THESE MOONLIT RIDDLES TO UNLOCK THE
SECRETS OF VARIANCE, JUST LIKE LUNA DID.

I'M A GLITTERING JEWEL
IN THE NIGHT SKY, BUT
I'M NOT A DIAMOND.
WHAT AM I?

_____

I VANISH DURING THE DAY
BUT GLOW AT NIGHT,
PROVIDING SOFT LIGHT.
WHAT AM I?

_____

I'M A FLEETING STREAK
OF LIGHT ACROSS THE SKY,
MAKING WISHES COME
TRUE.
WHAT AM I?

_____

I COME IN MANY SHAPES
AND SIZES, FLOATING HIGH
ABOVE.
WHAT AM I?

_____

I'M A CONSTELLATION
THAT LOOKS LIKE A
HUNTER.
WHAT AM I?

_____

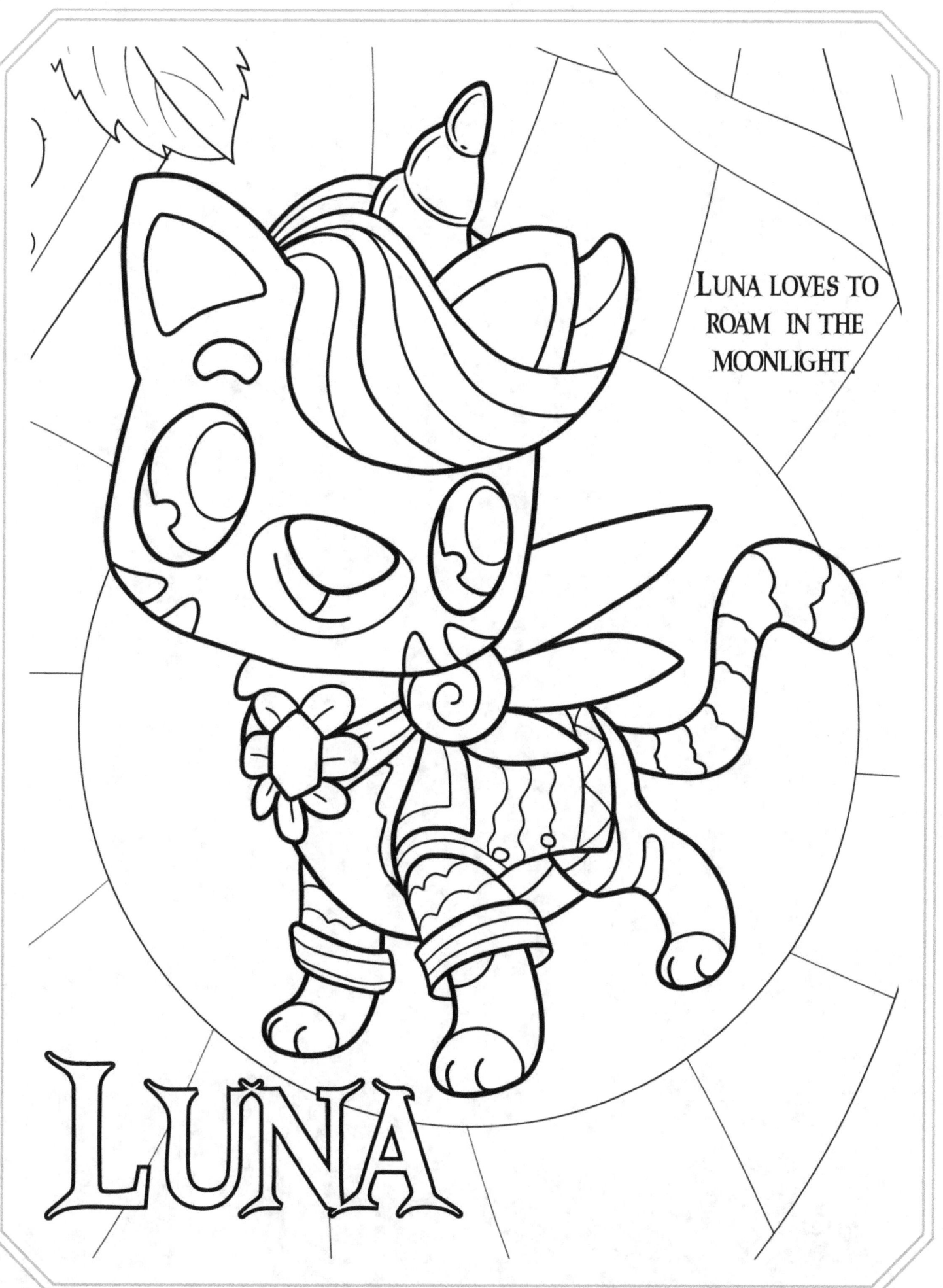

LUNA LOVES TO
ROAM IN THE
MOONLIGHT.

LUNA

Completed By:

Date:

ALD

THE ADVENTUROUS PARROT

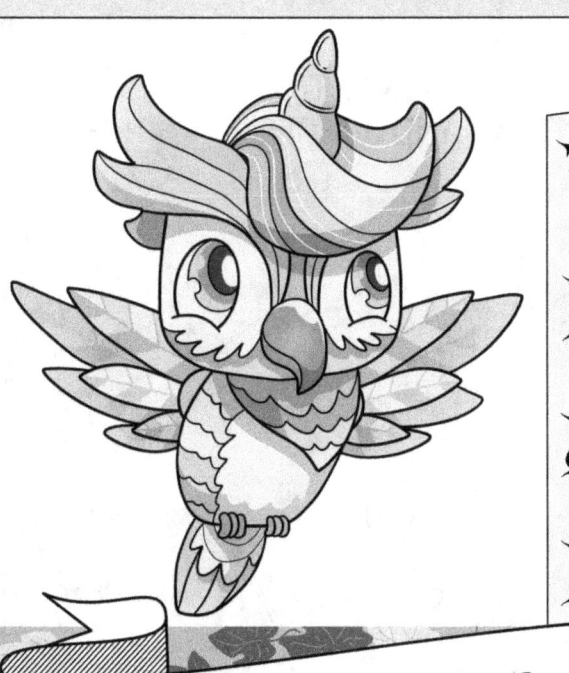

TRAITS: ADVENTUROUS, TALKATIVE, COLORFUL.

LIKES: SOARING THROUGH THE SKIES, LEARNING NEW LANGUAGES, SHARING STORIES.

DISLIKES: BEING CAGED, BORING CONVERSATIONS, STAYING IN ONE PLACE.

FUN FACT: ALD CAN MIMIC THE SOUNDS OF OTHER CREATURES IN VARIANCE!

ALD'S SOARING SONG

IN THE LAND OF VARIANCE, WHERE MELODIES MINGLED WITH THE WIND, LIVED ALD THE MELODIOUS PARROT. WITH COLORFUL FEATHERS THAT MIRRORED A RAINBOW,

ALD HAD A GIFT THAT ENCHANTED ALL WHO HEARD — A VOICE THAT TURNED FEELINGS INTO SONGS. ONE DAY, A GENTLE BREEZE CARRIED ALD'S SONG BEYOND THE BORDERS OF VARIANCE, TOUCHING HEARTS NEAR AND FAR. ALD EMBARKED ON A MUSICAL JOURNEY, SHARING SONGS OF JOY, COURAGE, AND FRIENDSHIP. THE WORLD RESONATED WITH ALD'S MELODIES, AND THROUGH HIS VOICE, VARIANCE'S HARMONY EXTENDED ITS EMBRACE.

MUSICAL HARMONY
EMBRACE THE MAGIC OF MUSIC WITH ALD!

COLOR THE MUSICAL NOTES AND INSTRUMENTS,
ADDING YOUR OWN UNIQUE PATTERNS AND SHADES.

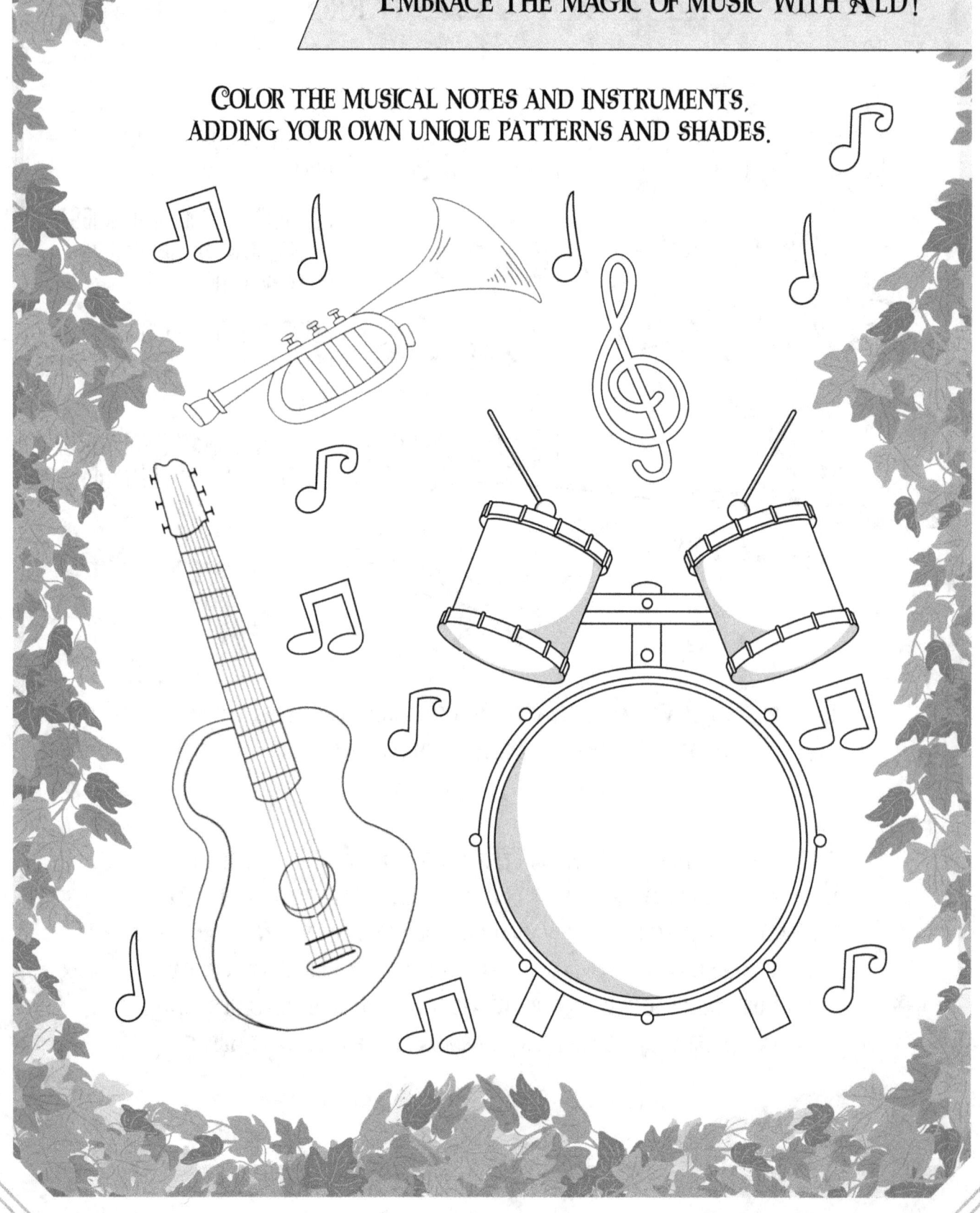

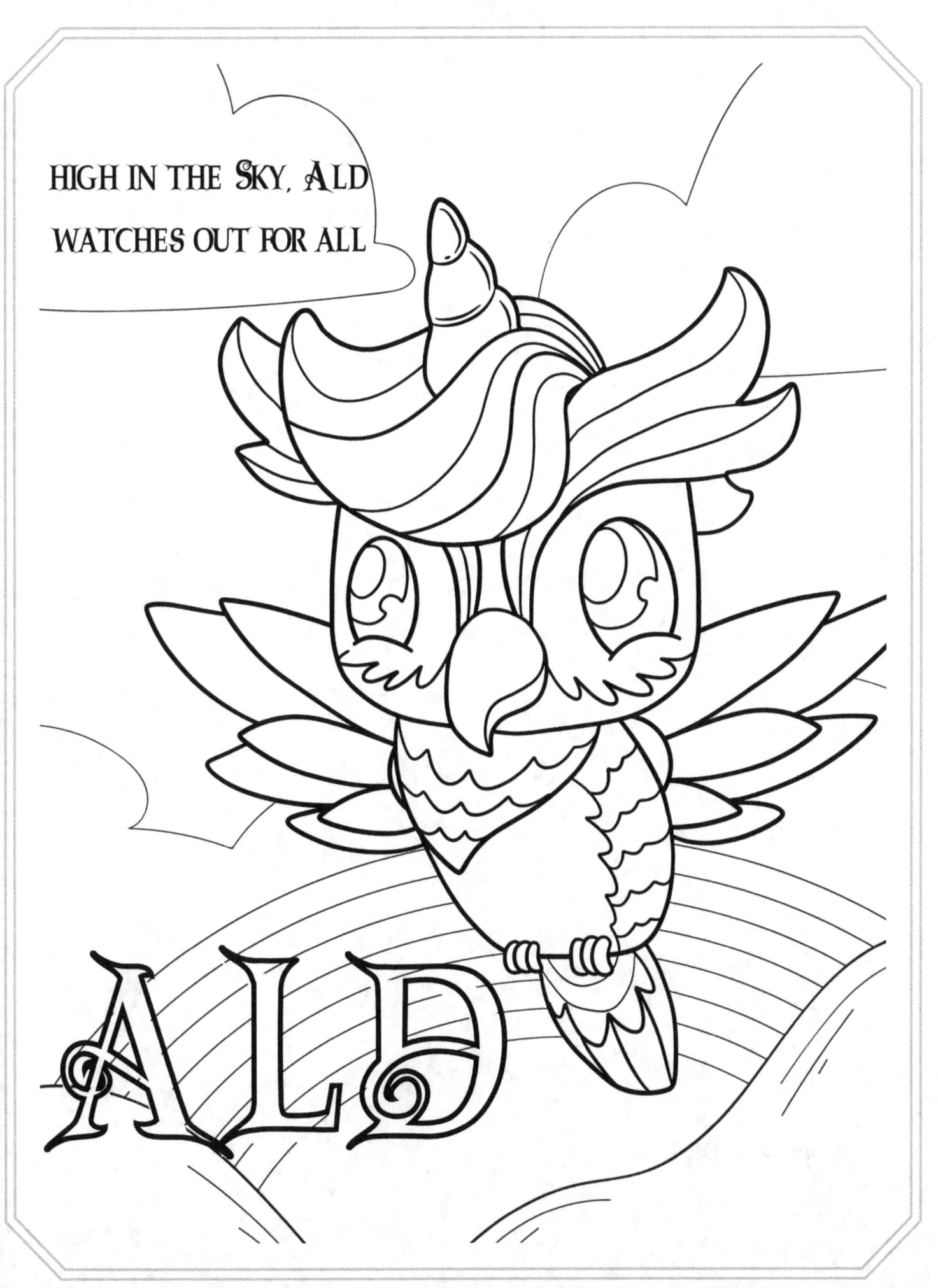

Completed By:

Date:

DEE

THE JOYFUL KOALA

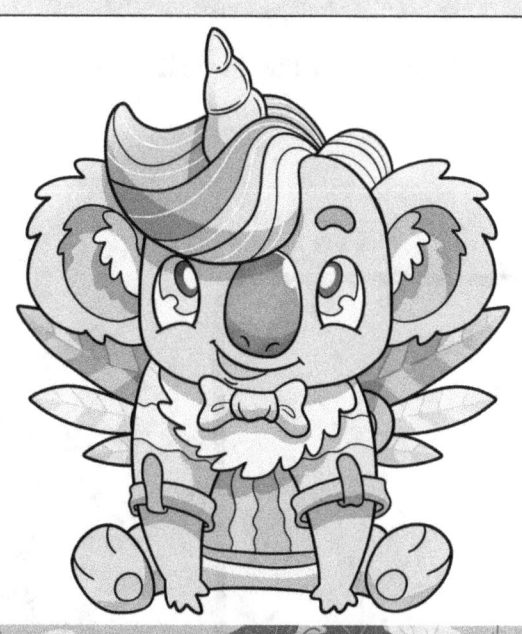

TRAITS: JOYFUL, RELAXED, GENTLE.

LIKES: NAPPING IN TREES, MUNCHING ON EUCALYPTUS LEAVES, SHARING HUGS.

DISLIKES: LOUD NOISES, FAST MOVEMENTS, CROWDED SPACES.

FUN FACT: DEE'S FLUFFY FUR IS THE COZIEST SPOT IN ALL OF VARIANCE!

DEE'S DELIGHTFUL DISCOVERY

IN THE ENCHANTING LAND OF VARIANCE, WHERE EUCALYPTUS LEAVES WHISPERED SECRETS, DEE THE KOALA EMBARKED ON A DELIGHTFUL ADVENTURE. KNOWN FOR HER GENTLE SPIRIT, DEE OFTEN SOUGHT MOMENTS OF TRANQUILITY AMIDST THE LUSH TREES. ONE DAY, WHILE EXPLORING, SHE STUMBLED UPON A HIDDEN WATERFALL GLISTENING LIKE A PRECIOUS GEM. ENTRANCED BY ITS BEAUTY, DEE FELT A SURGE OF INSPIRATION. SHE GATHERED LEAVES, STICKS, AND PEBBLES, CREATING INTRICATE SCULPTURES THAT CELEBRATED THE WATERFALL'S MAGIC. DEE'S ARTISTRY TRANSFORMED THE SURROUNDINGS INTO AN ENCHANTING GALLERY, CAPTURING THE WONDER OF VARIANCE FOR ALL TO ADMIRE.

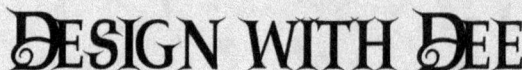

DESIGN WITH DEE

UNLEASH YOUR INNER ARTIST WITH DEE!

DRAW NATURE-THEMED SCULPTURES WITH ELEMENTS FROM THE STORY AND BRING DEE'S CREATIVE VISION TO LIFE.

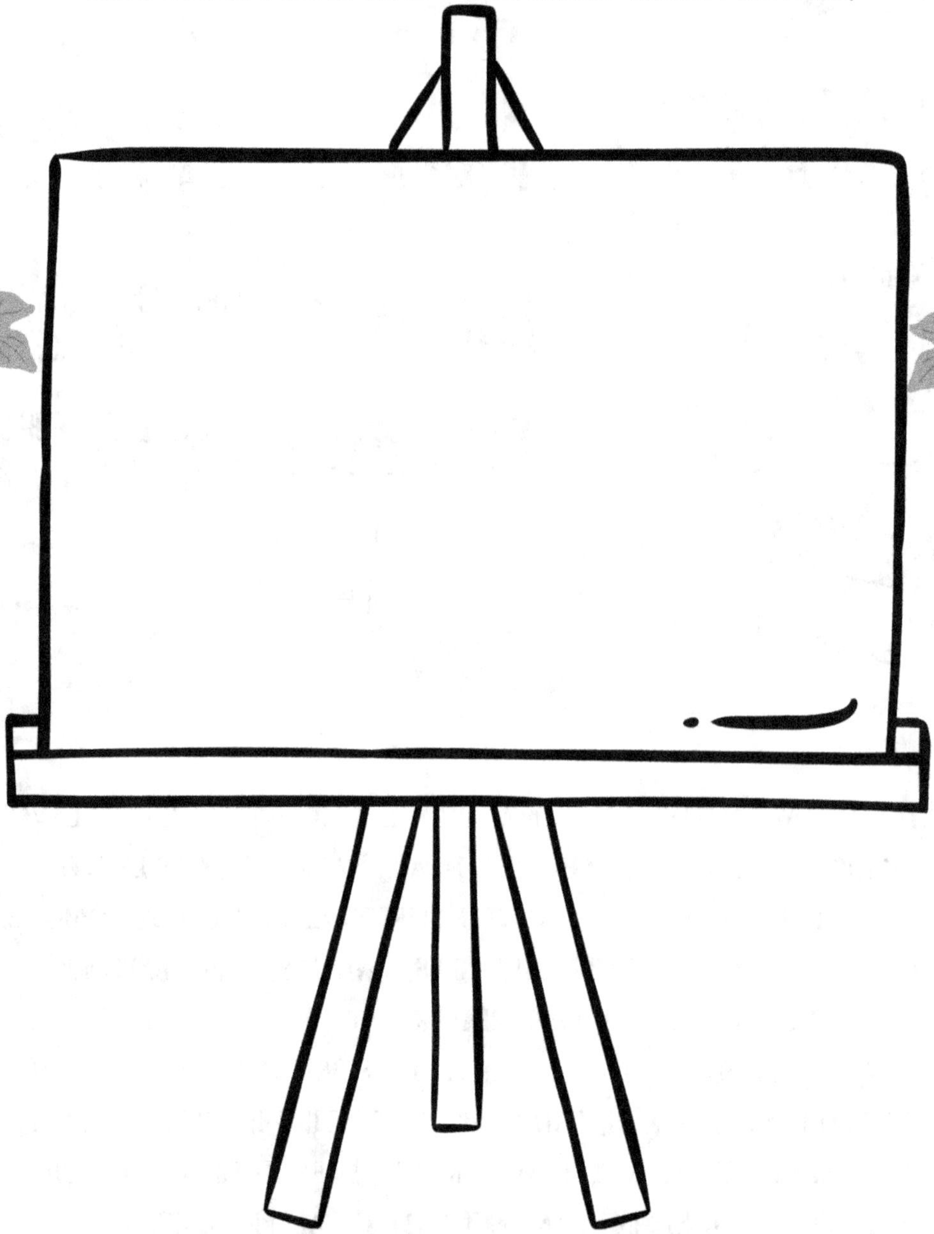

DRAW LEAVES, STICKS, AND PEBBLES TO COMPLETE DEE'S SCULPTURES.
ADD VIBRANT COLORS TO THE NATURAL ELEMENTS, SHOWCASING YOUR ARTISTIC FLAIR.

DEE

Dee sits high in the tree talking with friends.

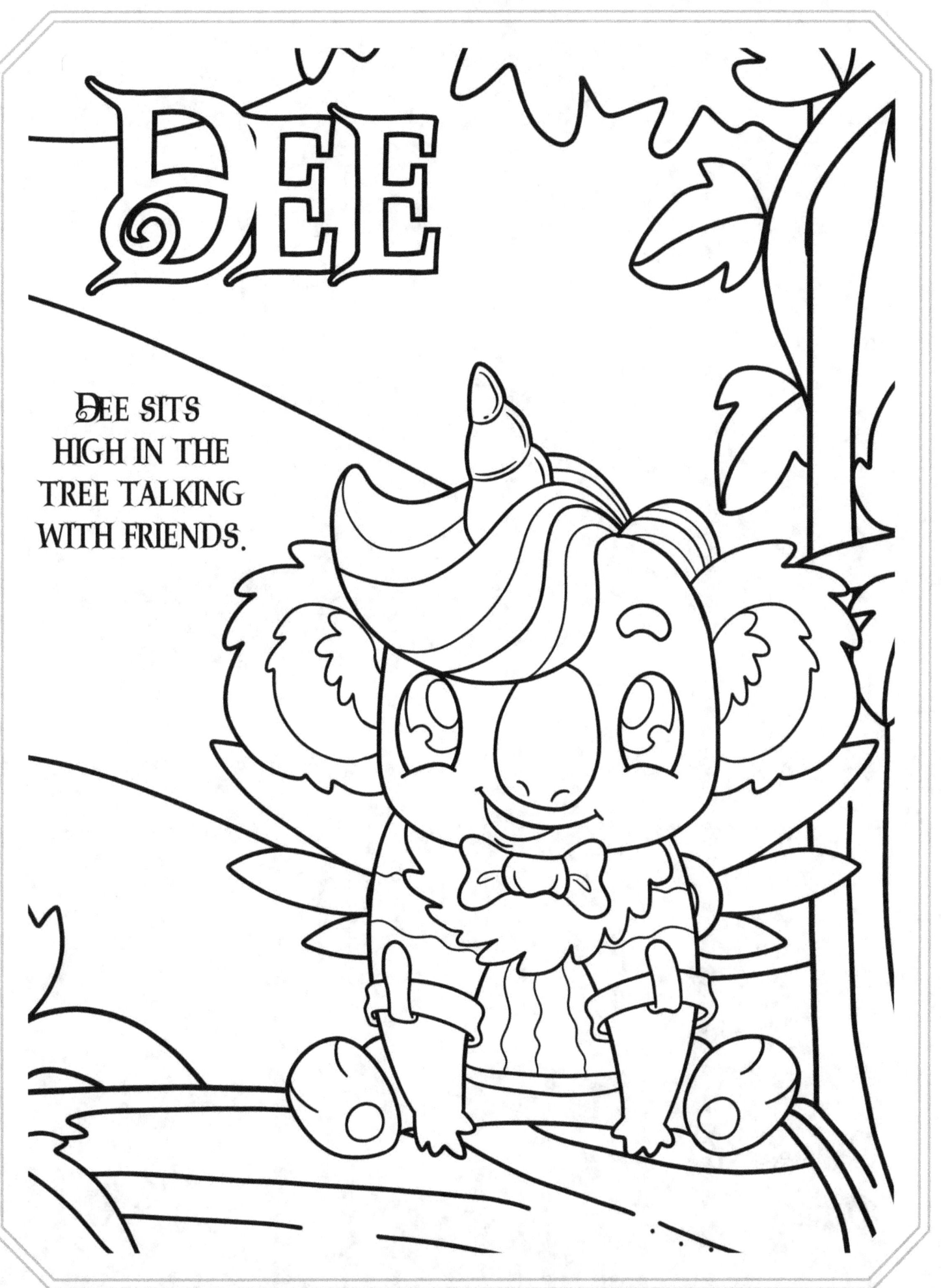

Completed By:

Date:

TANTAN

THE PLAYFUL PUPPY:

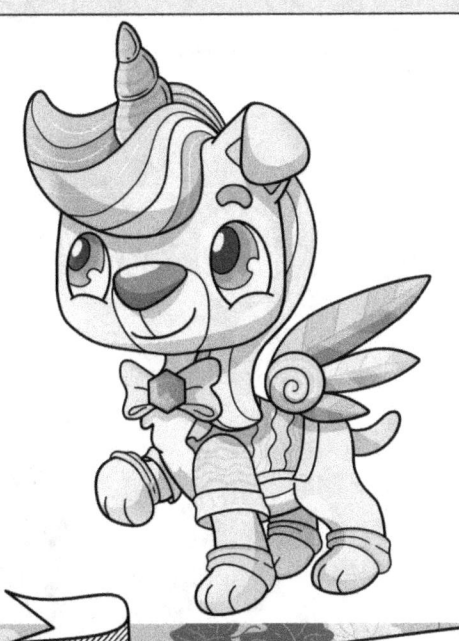

TRAITS: PLAYFUL, CURIOUS, LOYAL.

LIKES: CHASING BUTTERFLIES, DIGGING FOR TREASURES, FETCHING STICKS.

DISLIKES: BEING IGNORED, BEING ALONE, THORNY BUSHES.

FUN FACT: TANTAN'S TAIL WAGS SO FAST IT CAN CREATE A BREEZE!

TANTAN'S PLAYFUL PURSUIT

IN THE WHIMSICAL LAND OF VARIANCE, WHERE LAUGHTER ECHOED THROUGH THE MEADOWS, TANTAN THE PLAYFUL PUPPY WAS ALWAYS READY FOR FUN. ONE SUNNY DAY, TANTAN DISCOVERED A TRAIL OF BOUNCING BUBBLES, EACH CARRYING A SECRET SURPRISE. WITH BOUNDLESS ENERGY, TANTAN CHASED THE BUBBLES, DISCOVERING HIDDEN TREASURES ALONG THE WAY — A SPARKLING PEBBLE, A SHINY FEATHER, AND EVEN A RAINBOW-HUED LEAF. TANTAN'S TAIL WAGGED WITH DELIGHT AS HE REALIZED THAT JOY COULD BE FOUND IN THE SIMPLEST OF MOMENTS. FROM THEN ON, TANTAN SPREAD HAPPINESS BY LEAVING BEHIND TRAILS OF BUBBLES, REMINDING EVERYONE OF THE MAGIC IN PLAY.

CREATE YOUR BUBBLES

DRAW AND COLOR YOUR OWN SURPRISES IN THE BUBBLES!

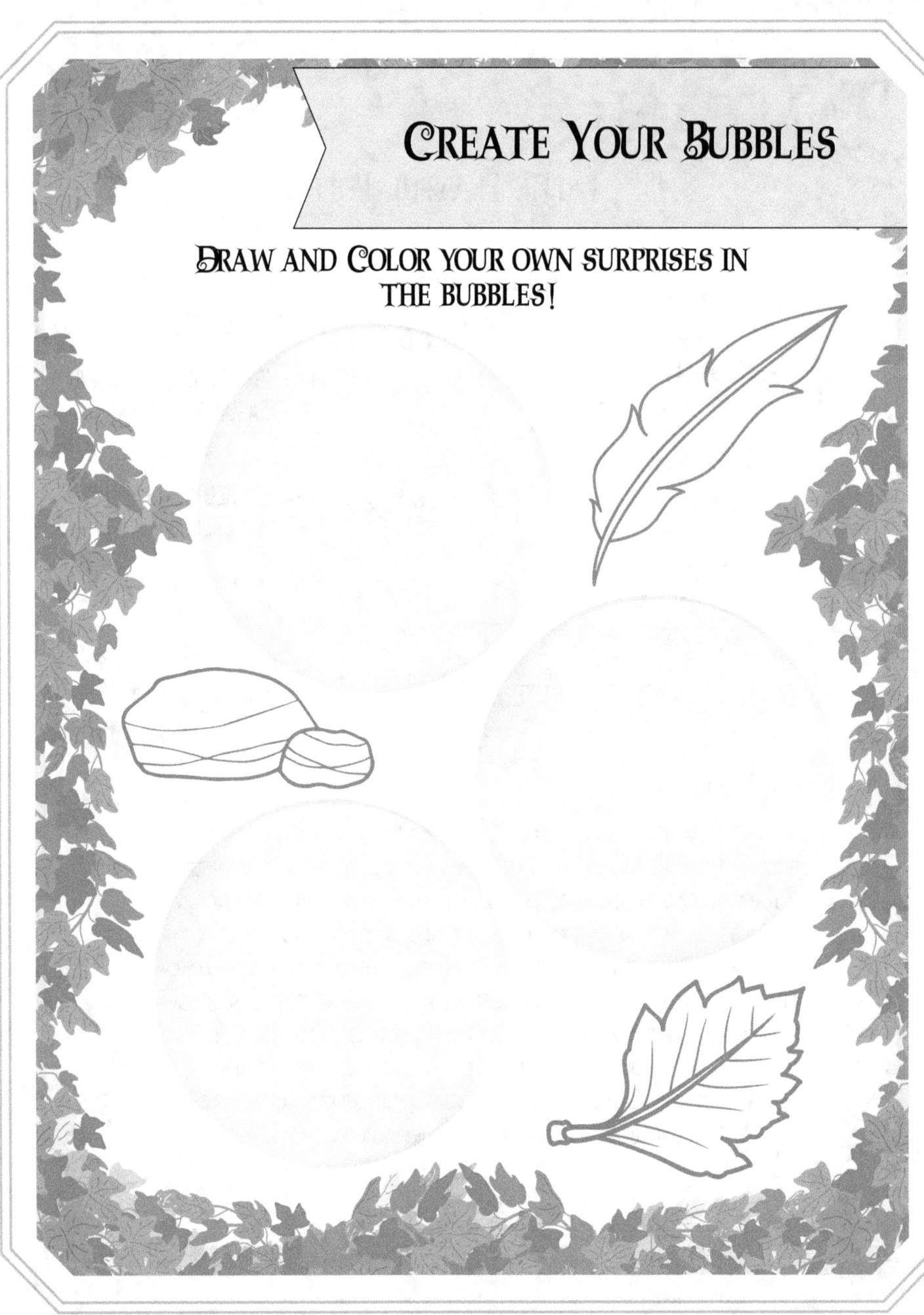

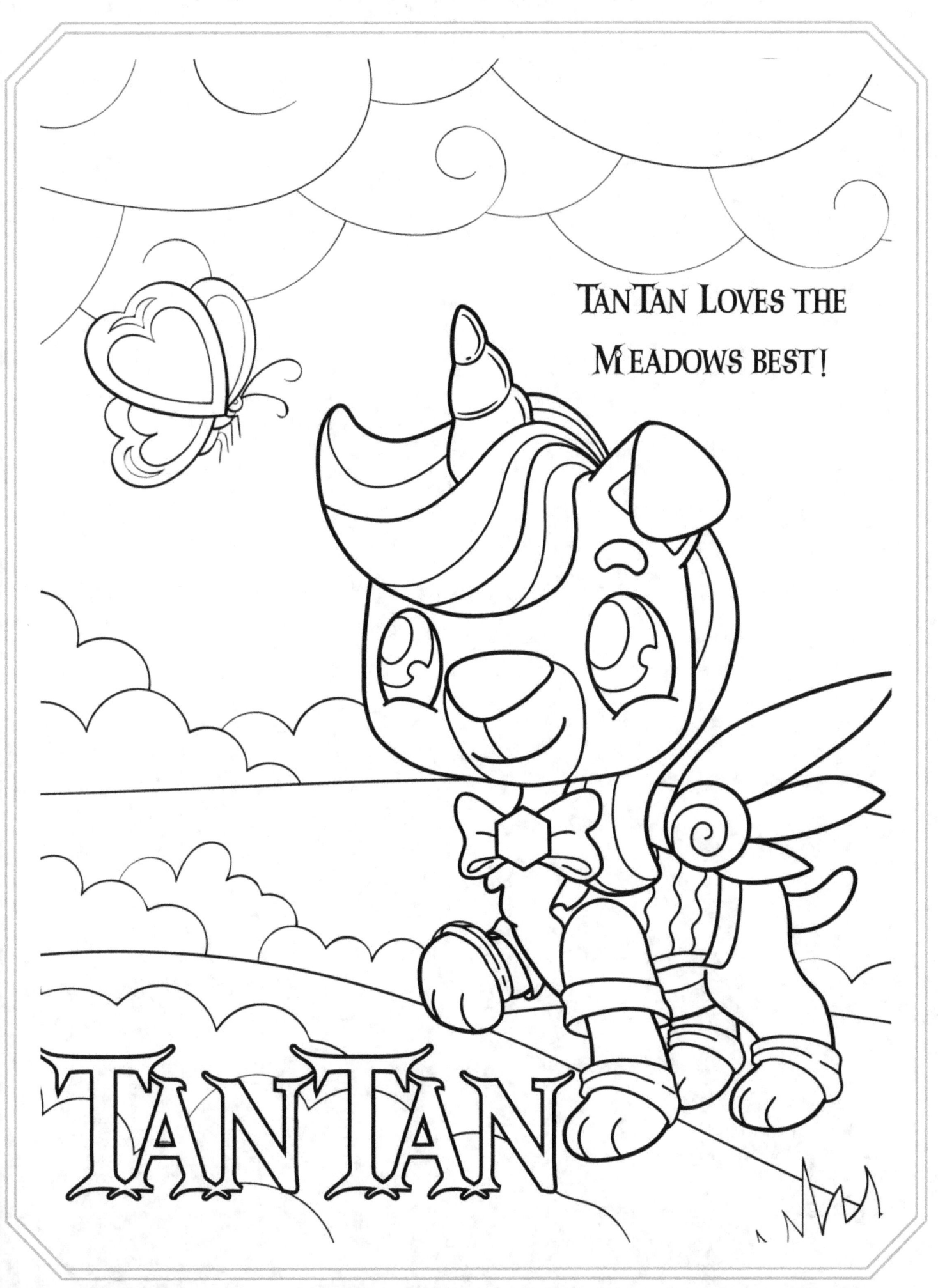

Completed By:

Date:

LOTUS

THE FROLICSOME FROG

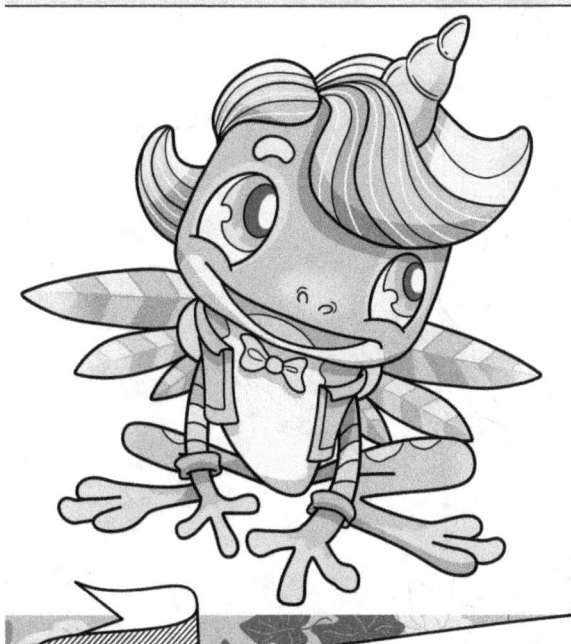

TRAITS: FROLICSOME, FRIENDLY, CURIOUS.

LIKES: LEAPING FROM LILY PAD TO LILY PAD, CROAKING IN HARMONY, EXPLORING PONDS.

DISLIKES: DRY LAND, BEING STUCK IN ONE PLACE, NOISY DISRUPTIONS.

FUN FACT: LOTUS CAN LEAP HIGHER THAN ANY OTHER FROG IN VARIANCE!

LOTUS AND THE ENCHANTED POND

IN THE SERENE LAND OF VARIANCE, WHERE NATURE'S SECRETS BLOOMED, LOTUS THE CONTEMPLATIVE FROG DWELLED BY A TRANQUIL POND. ONE MISTY MORNING, LOTUS GAZED INTO THE SHIMMERING WATERS AND NOTICED A REFLECTION THAT WASN'T HER OWN — A BEAUTIFUL, RADIANT FLOWER. INTRIGUED, LOTUS LEAPED INTO THE POND, ONLY TO FIND HERSELF IN AN UNDERWATER REALM. SURROUNDED BY VIBRANT FLORA AND SHIMMERING FISH, LOTUS EMBARKED ON AN UNDERWATER EXPLORATION. SHE UNCOVERED HIDDEN TREASURES AND ENCOUNTERED MYSTICAL CREATURES, EACH WITH A LESSON TO SHARE. RETURNING TO HER POND, LOTUS BROUGHT THE WISDOM OF THE UNDERWATER WORLD TO VARIANCE'S SURFACE, INSPIRING GROWTH, LEARNING, AND NEW BEGINNINGS.

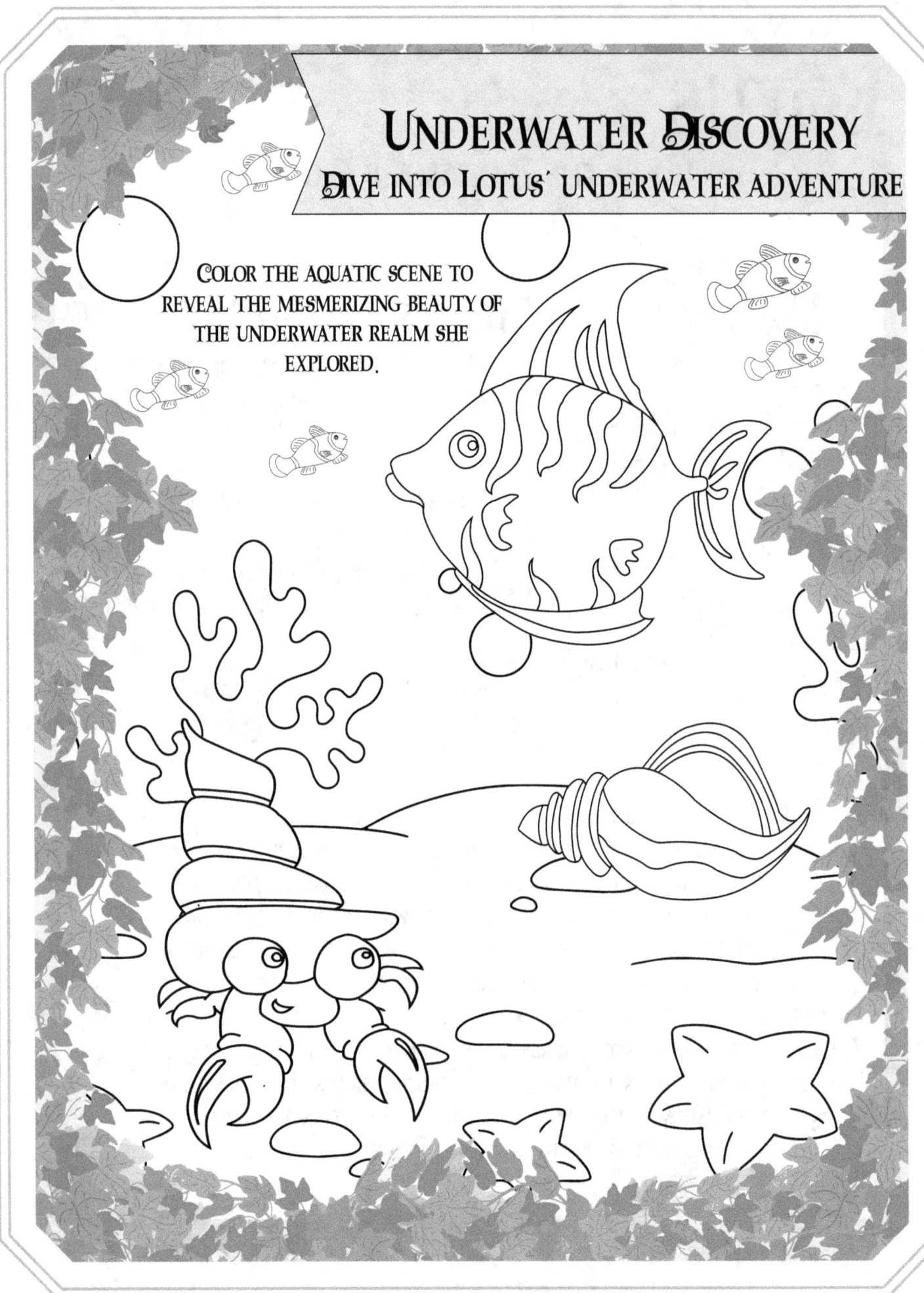

UNDERWATER DISCOVERY
DIVE INTO LOTUS' UNDERWATER ADVENTURE

COLOR THE AQUATIC SCENE TO REVEAL THE MESMERIZING BEAUTY OF THE UNDERWATER REALM SHE EXPLORED.

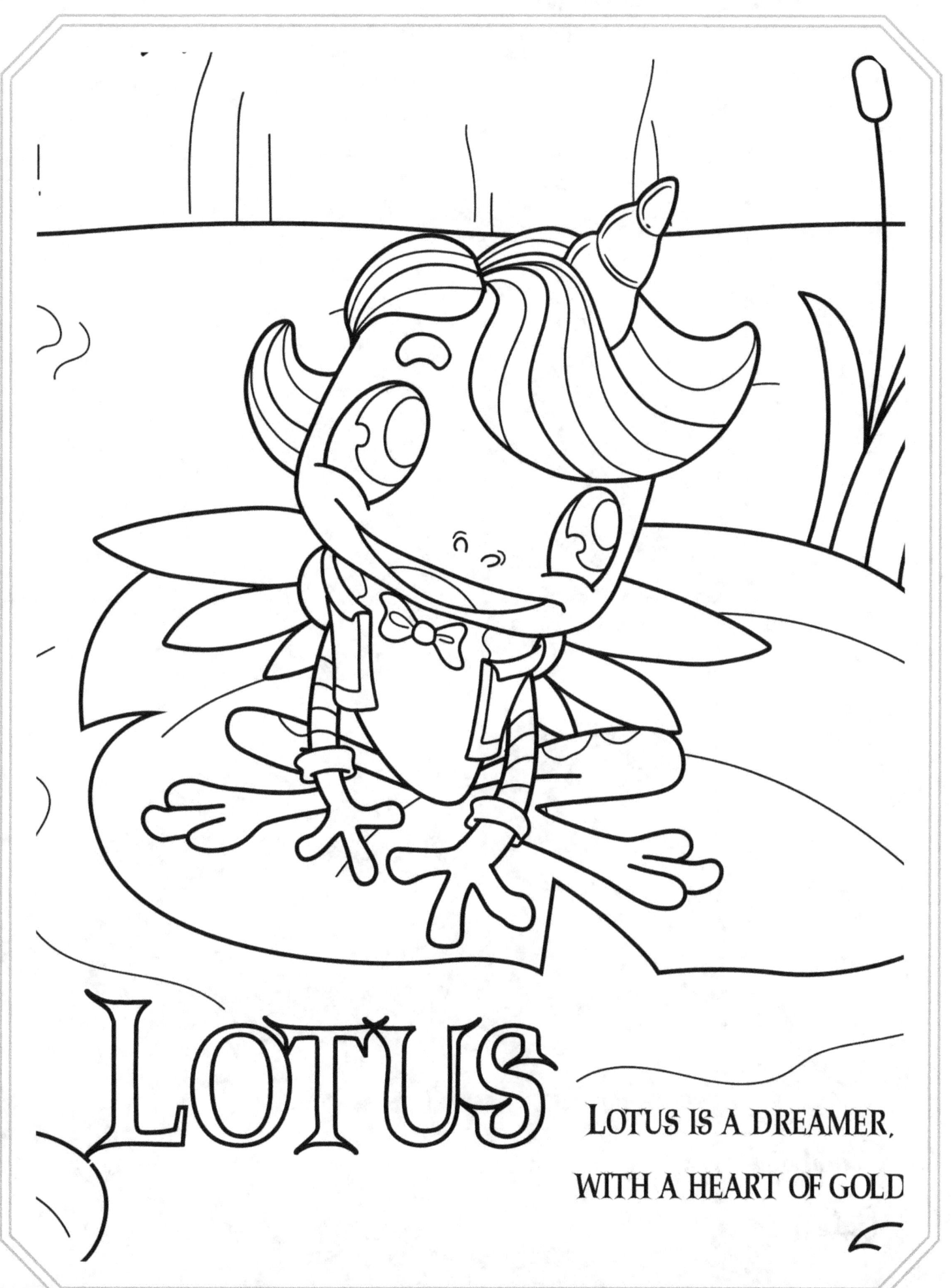

LOTUS

LOTUS IS A DREAMER,
WITH A HEART OF GOLD

Completed By:

Date:

OLLIE

THE FRIENDLY SEAL:

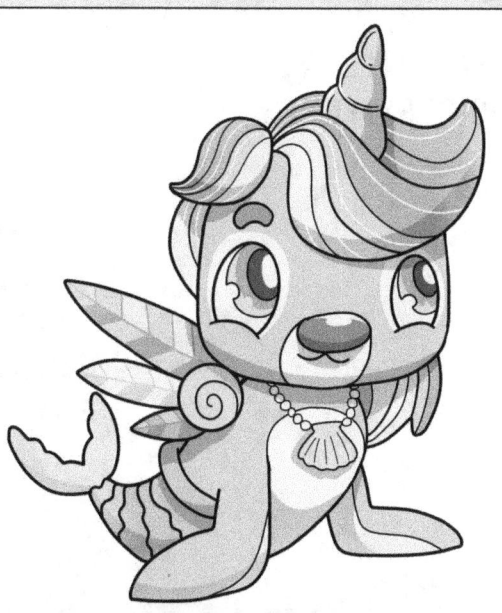

TRAITS: FRIENDLY, PLAYFUL, GRACEFUL.

LIKES: SPLASHING IN WAVES, SUNBATHING ON ROCKS, MAKING SANDCASTLES.

DISLIKES: COLD WEATHER, BEING ALONE, POLLUTED WATERS.

FUN FACT: OLLIE CAN BALANCE A PEARL ON ITS NOSE FOR HOURS!

OLLIE'S OCEANIC QUEST

IN THE ENCHANTING LAND OF VARIANCE, WHERE WAVES WHISPERED ANCIENT TALES, OLLIE THE ADVENTUROUS SEAL LONGED TO EXPLORE THE DEPTHS OF THE OCEAN. ONE MOONLIT NIGHT, A MYSTERIOUS SHELL APPEARED ON THE SHORE, ITS IRIDESCENT GLOW CALLING TO OLLIE'S HEART. WITH A JOYFUL FLIP, OLLIE DOVE INTO THE SEA, GUIDED BY THE SHELL'S ETHEREAL LIGHT. THROUGH CORAL REEFS AND SHIMMERING CAVES, OLLIE SWAM ALONGSIDE GENTLE SEA CREATURES AND UNRAVELED THE OCEAN'S SECRETS. AT LAST, THE SHELL LED OLLIE TO A SUNKEN SHIP, WHERE A TREASURE CHEST BRIMMING WITH STORIES AWAITED. OLLIE EMERGED FROM THE OCEAN, NOT ONLY WITH STORIES TO SHARE, BUT ALSO WITH A NEWFOUND UNDERSTANDING OF THE PROFOUND CONNECTIONS THAT LINKED ALL OF VARIANCE'S INHABITANTS.

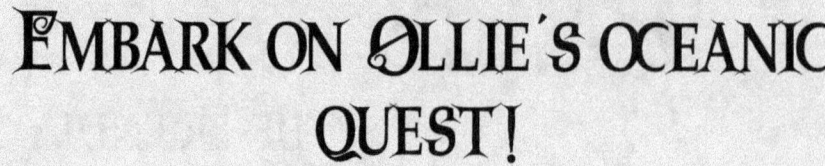

EMBARK ON OLLIE'S OCEANIC QUEST!

DRAW THE SHIMMERING CAVES AND GENTLE SEA
CREATURES ENCOUNTERS OLLIE AS SHE EXPLORES.

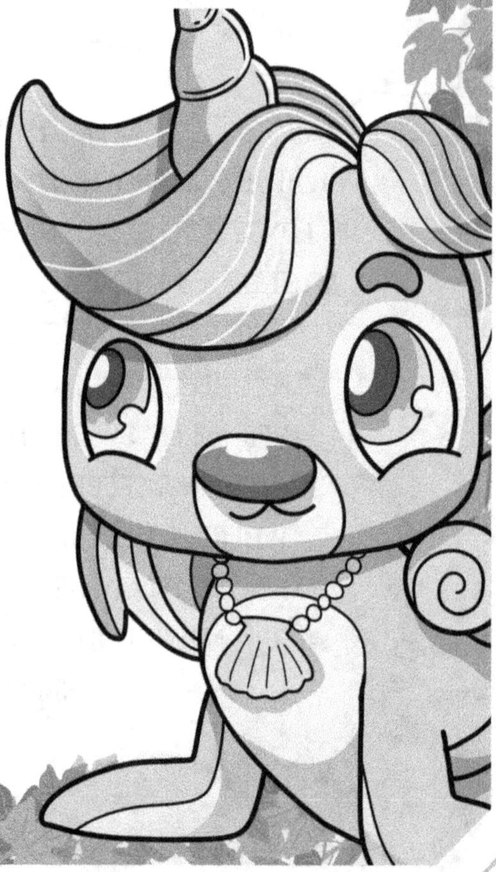

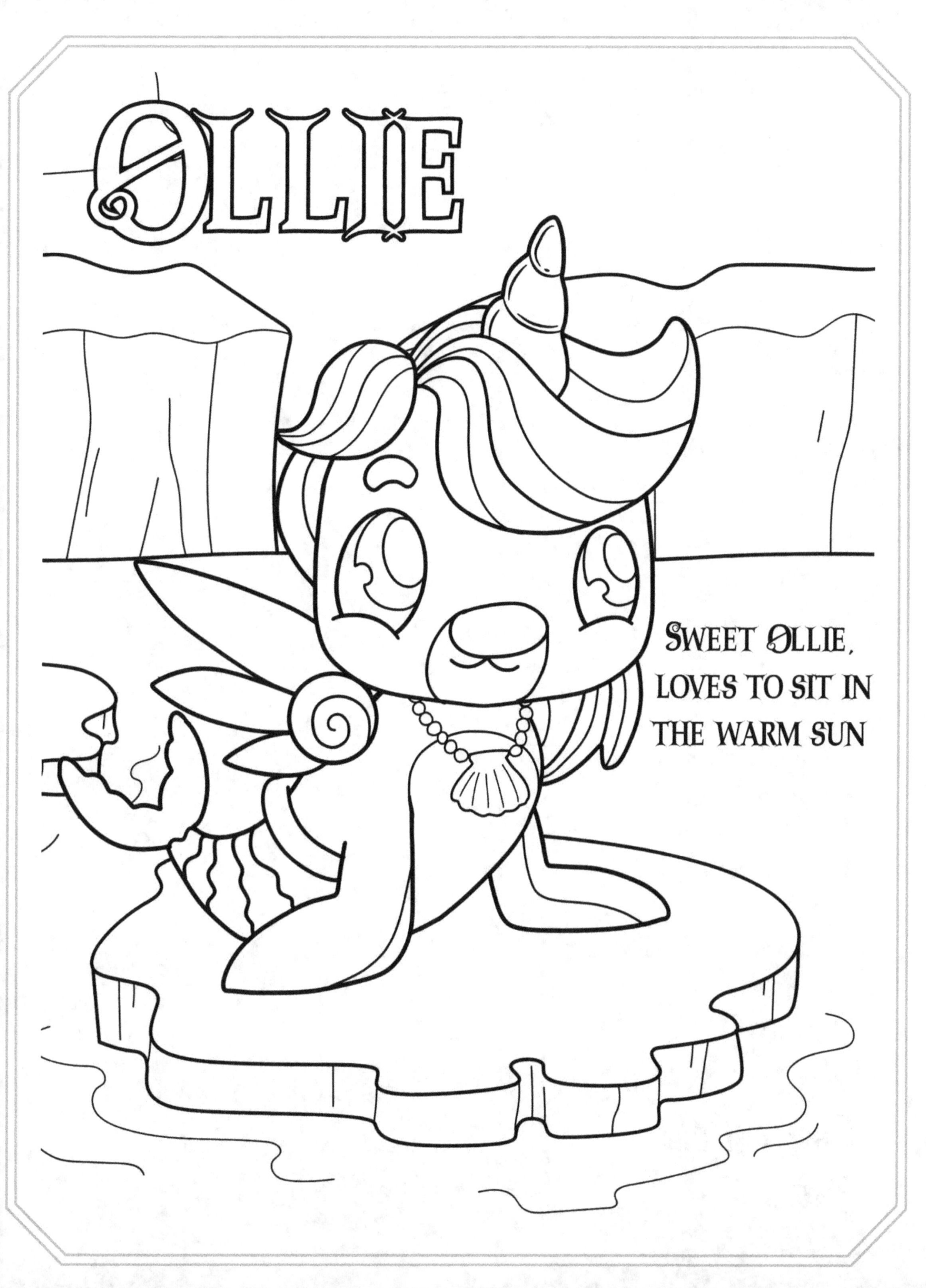

Completed By:

Date:

LUCKY
THE STRATEGIC PENGUIN

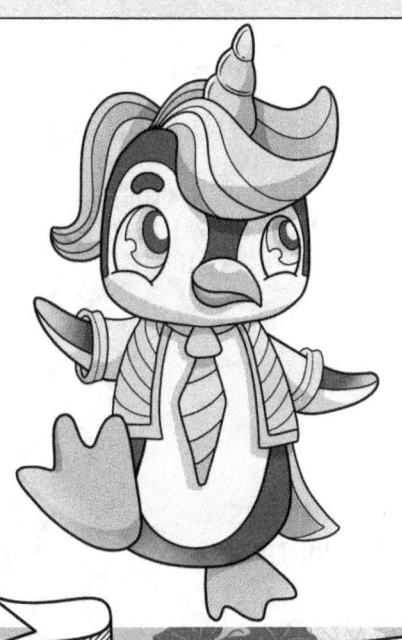

TRAITS: STRATEGIC, RESOURCEFUL, OBSERVANT.

LIKES: NAVIGATING ICY MAZES, OBSERVING STAR PATTERNS, SOLVING TRICKY PUZZLES.

DISLIKES: CHAOTIC SITUATIONS, FEELING LOST, RUSHING WITHOUT A PLAN.

FUN FACT: LUCKY HAS A KNACK FOR FINDING THE PERFECT PATH, EVEN IN THE FOGGIEST CONDITIONS!

LUCKY'S STRATEGIC SEARCH

IN THE MESMERIZING LAND OF VARIANCE, WHERE PUZZLES DANCED ON THE WIND, LUCKY THE STRATEGIC PENGUIN HELD A UNIQUE POWER — THE ABILITY TO DECIPHER RIDDLES AND SOLVE MYSTERIES. ONE CHILLY DAY, A MAP WITH INTRICATE CLUES APPEARED AT LUCKY'S DOORSTEP. WITH A DETERMINED WADDLE, LUCKY EMBARKED ON A STRATEGIC SEARCH, UNRAVELING EACH CLUE TO REVEAL HIDDEN TREASURES. ALONG THE WAY, LUCKY ENCOUNTERED ANCIENT SCROLLS, ENIGMATIC SYMBOLS, AND CLEVERLY CONCEALED COMPARTMENTS. AS THE FINAL PUZZLE PIECE CLICKED INTO PLACE, A MAGNIFICENT DISCOVERY AWAITED — NOT JUST A TREASURE, BUT THE REALIZATION THAT KNOWLEDGE AND STRATEGY WERE THE GREATEST REWARDS OF ALL.

LUCKY'S RIDDLE TIME

RIDDLE:

WITH TINY WINGS, I
FLUTTER AND FLY,
BRINGING JOY TO VARIANCE
AS I PASS BY.

WHAT CREATURE AM I?

RIDDLE:

I'M MADE OF WISHES AND
TWINKLING LIGHT,
AT NIGHT, I APPEAR,
SHINING SO BRIGHT.

WHAT LIGHTS UP
VARIANCE'S SKY?

RIDDLE:

I'M TALL AND GREEN,
A MAGICAL SIGHT,
IN VARIANCE'S
MEADOWS, I REACH A
GREAT HEIGHT,

WHO AM I?

REMEMBER HOW LUCKY SOLVED INTRICATE RIDDLES?
NOW IT'S YOUR TURN TO BECOME A MASTER RIDDLER!

THINK OF CLEVER RIDDLES THAT CHALLENGE YOUR FRIENDS' MINDS.
EACH RIDDLE SHOULD HAVE A HIDDEN ANSWER THAT'S RELATED TO SOMETHING
YOU BOTH KNOW!

RIDDLE:

_____

_____

ANSWER: _____

RIDDLE:

_____

_____

ANSWER: _____

RIDDLE:

_____

_____

ANSWER: _____

Answers: Butterfly, Stars and Tree.

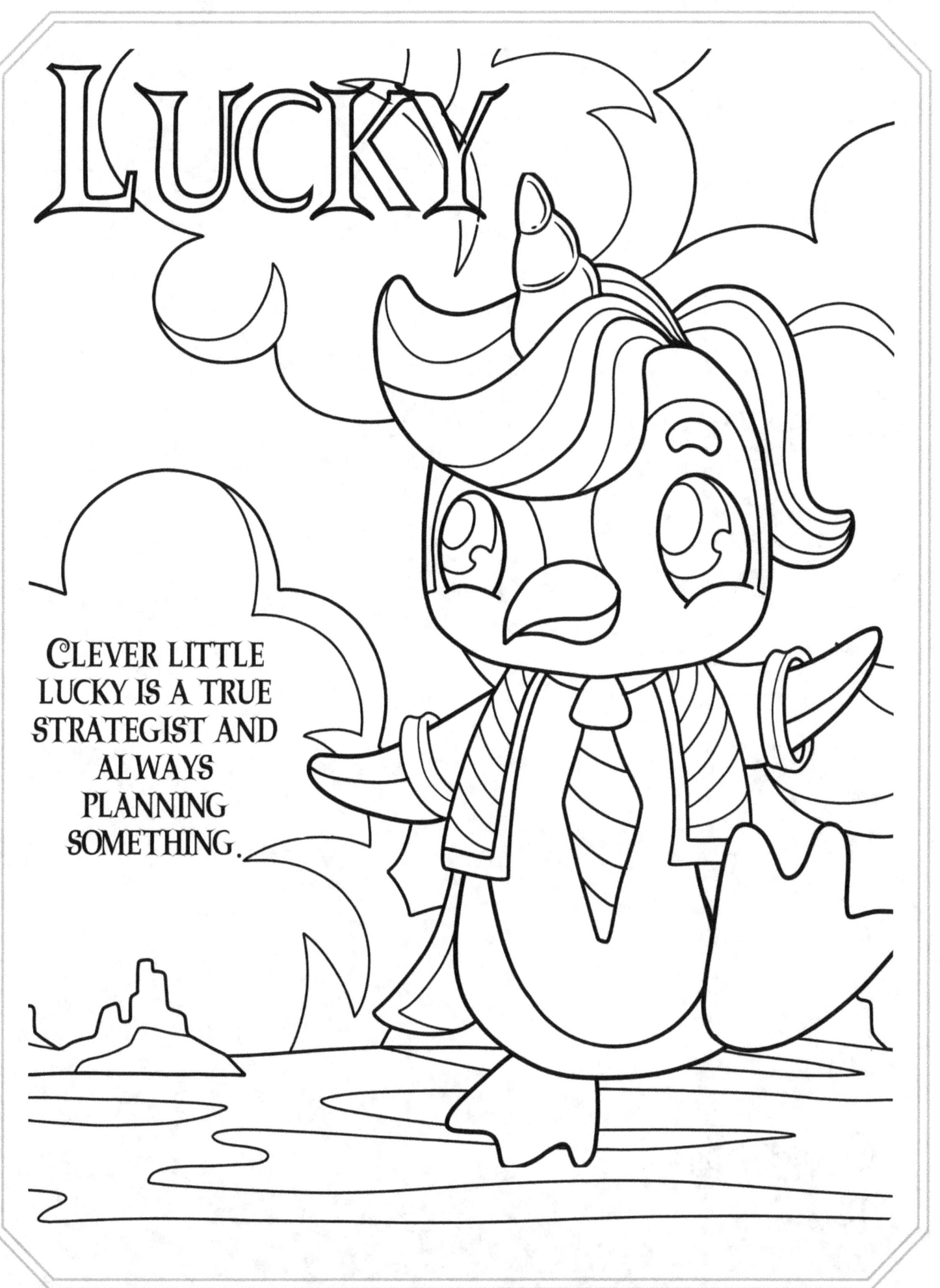

Completed By:

Date:

BANE
THE ROGUISH BUNNY

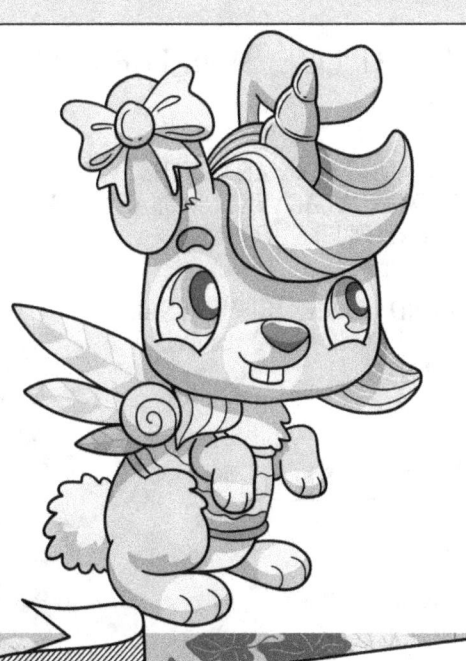

TRAITS: ROGUISH, ADVENTUROUS, CLEVER.

LIKES: EXPLORING HIDDEN NOOKS, HOPPING THROUGH MEADOWS, DISCOVERING SECRET SHORTCUTS.

DISLIKES: BEING CONFINED, PREDICTABLE PATHS, MISSING OUT ON EXCITING ESCAPADES.

FUN FACT: BANE'S BUNNY HOPS ARE FASTER THAN A LIGHTNING BOLT!

BANE'S MYSTERIOUS MAP

IN THE ENCHANTING LAND OF VARIANCE, WHERE SECRETS WHISPERED AMONG THE TREES, BANE THE ROGUISH BUNNY WAS KNOWN FOR HIS INSATIABLE CURIOSITY. ONE DAY, WHILE HOPPING THROUGH A MEADOW, BANE STUMBLED UPON AN OLD, WEATHERED MAP. INTRIGUED BY ITS FADED MARKINGS, HE SET OFF ON A DARING ADVENTURE. FOLLOWING THE MAP'S TWISTS AND TURNS, BANE ENCOUNTERED HIDDEN PATHS, MYSTERIOUS CAVES, AND SPARKLING GEMS. WITH EACH DISCOVERY, BANE'S HEART RACED WITH EXCITEMENT. THE JOURNEY LED HIM TO A LONG-FORGOTTEN TREASURE CHEST, FILLED NOT WITH GOLD, BUT WITH STORIES OF COURAGE AND THE THRILL OF EXPLORATION.

ACTIVITY: CREATE YOUR CURIOUS EXPLORER'S JOURNAL

ARE YOU READY TO BECOME A CURIOUS EXPLORER, JUST LIKE BANE THE BUNNY FROM THE LAND OF VARIANCE?

EXPLORERS ARE PEOPLE WHO LOVE TO DISCOVER NEW THINGS AND LEARN ABOUT THE WORLD AROUND THEM. BANE WAS A CURIOUS BUNNY WHO WENT ON EXCITING ADVENTURES, AND NOW IT'S YOUR TURN! WITH YOUR VERY OWN CURIOUS EXPLORER'S JOURNAL,

YOU CAN RECORD ALL THE AMAZING THINGS YOU FIND AND LEARN. THIS JOURNAL WILL BE LIKE A MAGICAL BOOK THAT KEEPS YOUR EXPLORATIONS ALIVE FOREVER. LET'S GET STARTED ON THIS FUN ADVENTURE!

TO BEGIN YOUR CURIOUS EXPLORER'S JOURNAL, YOU'LL NEED SOME THINGS:

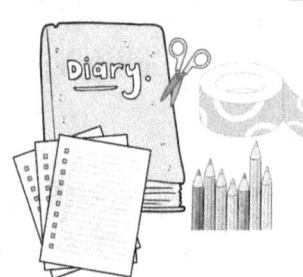

- A NOTEBOOK OR SOME SHEETS OF PAPER
- CRAYONS, COLORED PENCILS, OR MARKERS
- GLUE OR TAPE
- SCISSORS (WITH AN ADULT'S HELP)
- STICKERS, MAGAZINE PICTURES, OR ANY DECORATIONS YOU LIKE

DECORATE YOUR JOURNAL:

- MAKE YOUR JOURNAL SPECIAL! COLOR THE COVER WITH YOUR FAVORITE COLORS AND ADD STICKERS OR PICTURES TO MAKE IT UNIQUELY YOURS.
- WRITE YOUR NAME ON THE FIRST PAGE.
- USE YOUR CRAYONS OR GLUE TO ADD PICTURES OF WHAT YOU DISCOVER. DRAW FLOWERS, TREES, ANIMALS, OR ANYTHING THAT CATCHES YOUR EYE. YOU CAN ALSO GLUE SMALL ITEMS LIKE LEAVES, FEATHERS, OR EVEN A TINY ROCK!

A JOURNAL IS LIKE A TREASURE MAP OF YOUR EXPLORATIONS. KEEP ADDING NEW ENTRIES WHENEVER YOU FIND SOMETHING INTERESTING. WHO KNOWS WHAT YOU MIGHT DISCOVER NEXT?

WRITE ABOUT WHAT YOU CAN SEE, HEAR, TOUCH, AND EVEN SMELL DURING YOUR EXPLORATIONS. IMAGINE YOU'RE TELLING YOUR JOURNAL EVERYTHING THAT'S HAPPENING AROUND YOU!

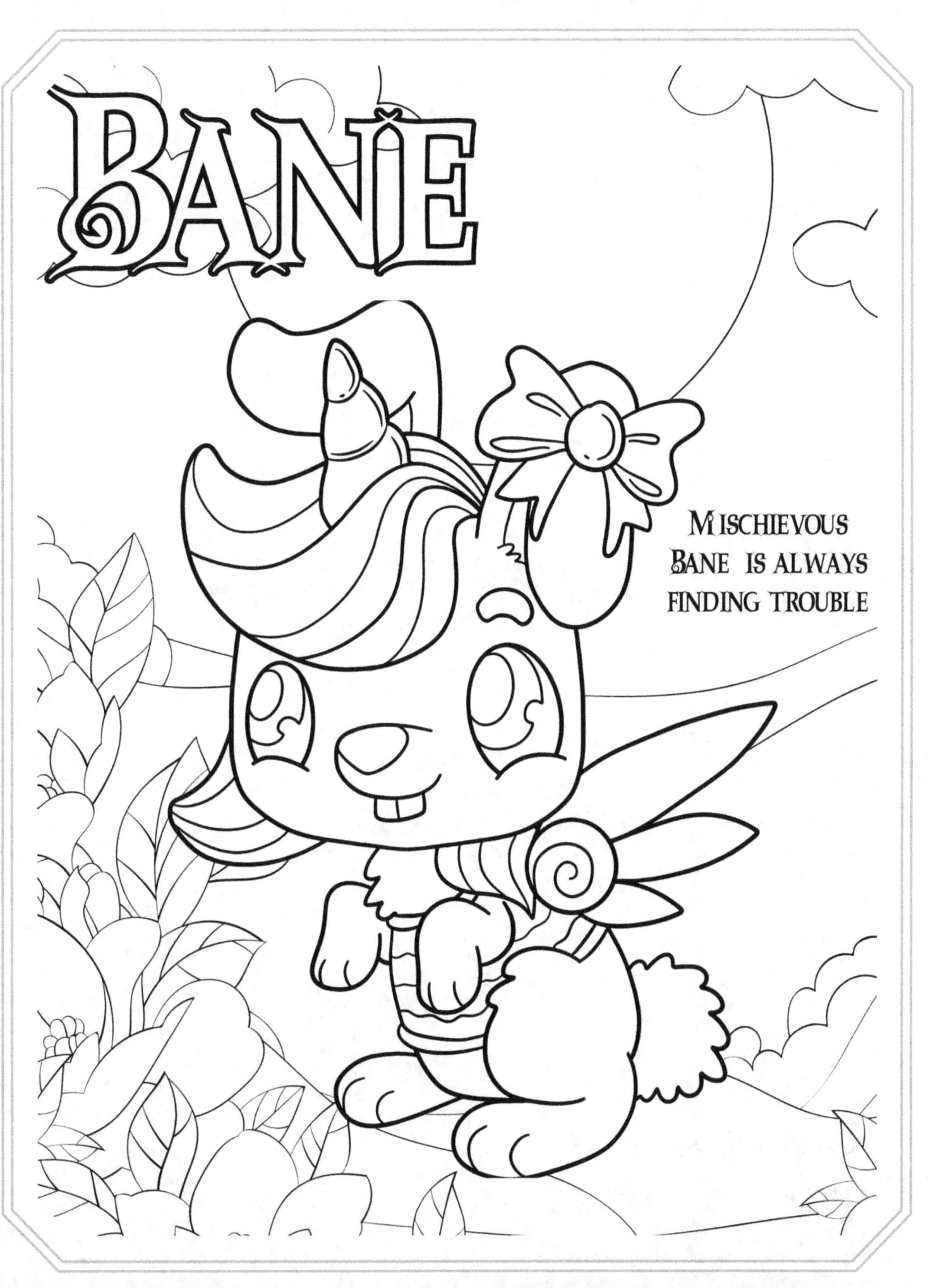

Completed By:

Date:

CHAROON

THE PLAYFUL LIMA:

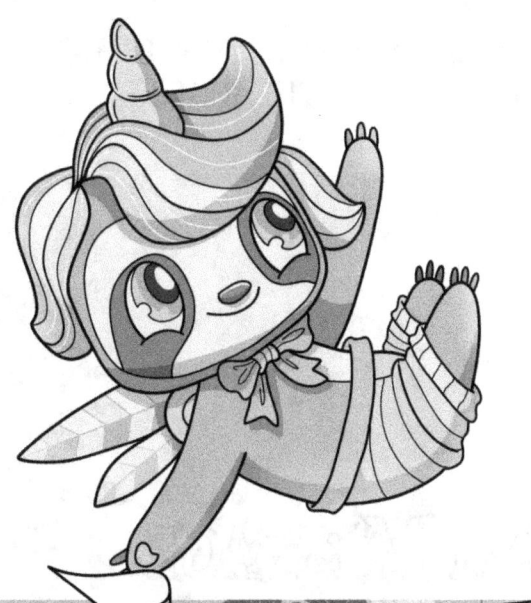

TRAITS: PLAYFUL, ENERGETIC, CURIOUS

LIKES: SKIPPING THROUGH FIELDS, DISCOVERING HIDDEN TREASURES, MAKING NEW FRIENDS

DISLIKES: STANDING STILL, BORING ROUTINES, RAINY DAYS

FUN FACT: CHAROON HAS A COLLECTION OF COLORFUL STONES FROM ALL AROUND VARIANCE!

CHAROON'S DARING DANCE

IN THE VIBRANT LAND OF VARIANCE, WHERE RHYTHM ECHOED IN THE AIR, CHAROON THE LIVELY LIMA WAS A DANCE ENTHUSIAST LIKE NO OTHER. WITH EVERY SWISH OF HIS TAIL AND FLUTTER OF HIS WINGS, CHAROON TRANSFORMED THE WORLD INTO HIS DANCE FLOOR. ONE SUNLIT DAY, A MESMERIZING MELODY DRIFTED THROUGH THE BREEZE, GUIDING CHAROON TO A HIDDEN GLADE. HERE, CHAROON ENCOUNTERED A GROUP OF WOODLAND CREATURES PREPARING FOR A GRAND DANCE CELEBRATION. CHAROON'S ENTHUSIASM WAS CONTAGIOUS, AND HE JOINED IN, ADDING HIS OWN UNIQUE MOVES TO THE DANCE. THE GLADE ERUPTED IN JOYOUS MOVEMENT, EACH STEP A TESTAMENT TO CHAROON'S SPIRIT AND THE MAGIC OF DANCE.

CHALLENGE YOUR BRAIN WITH A CRYPTOGRAM! CHAROON LOVES DANCES AND MUSIC, AND HE HAS LEFT A SECRET MESSAGE FOR YOU. USE THE CODE KEY TO DECODE WHAT HE'S SAYING.

CODE KEY:

A = Đ
B = R
C = M
D = L
E = T
F = A
G = C
H = F
I = S
J = O
K = N
L = H
M = U
N = B
O = G
P = Y
Q = P
R = F
S = V
T = W
U = K
V = X
W = J
X = Q
Y = Z
Z = Z

CRYPTOGRAM MESSAGE:

LDUMT   NIOT   UO   BUT

IF   XDVMLIUC

ANSWER:

_____

_____

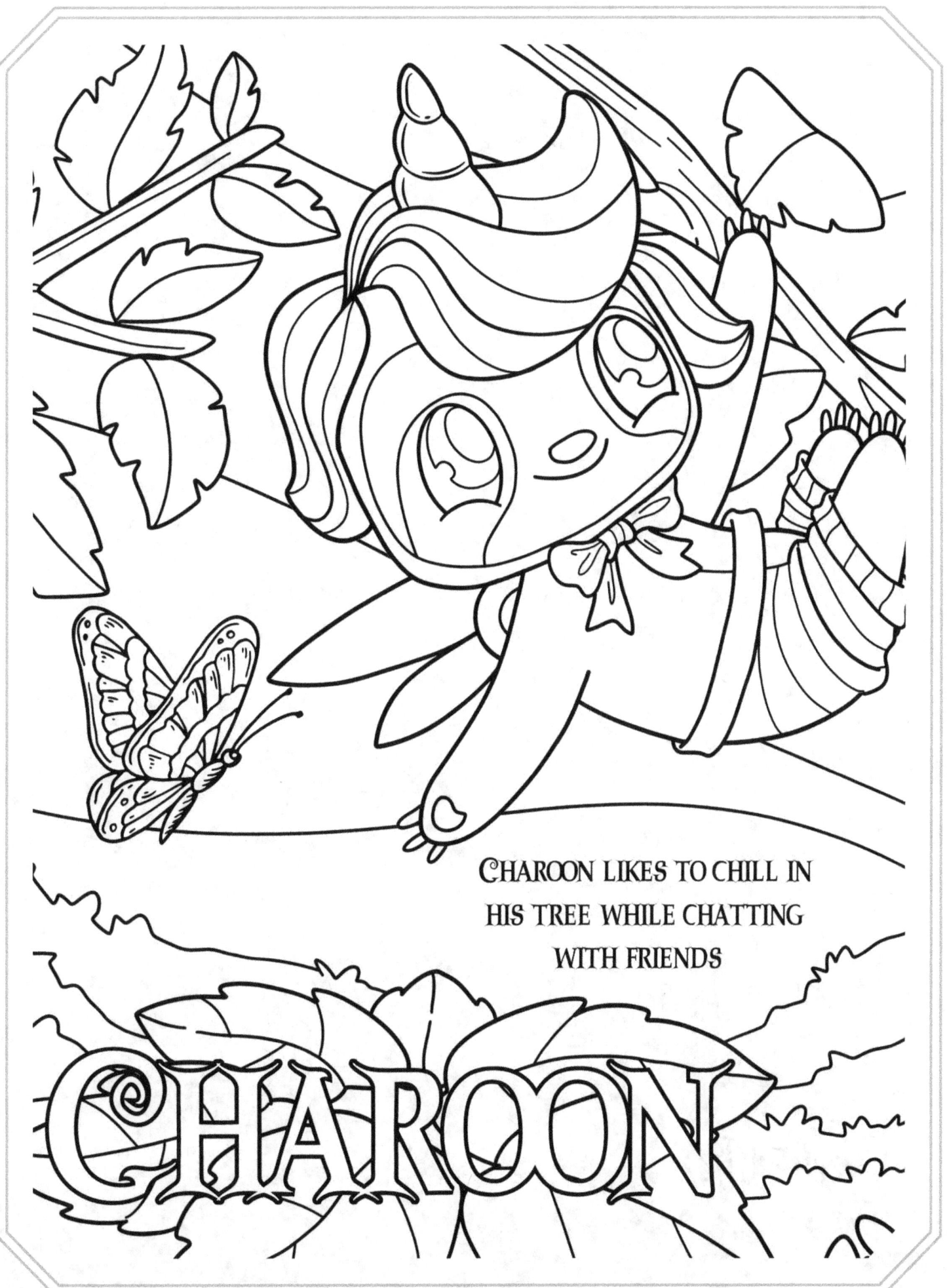

CHAROON LIKES TO CHILL IN
HIS TREE WHILE CHATTING
WITH FRIENDS

CHAROON

Completed By:

Date:

LESARA

THE STRONG RHINO

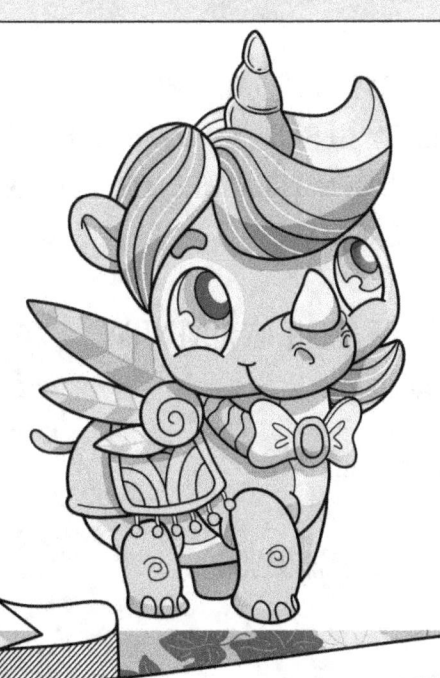

TRAITS: STRONG, DETERMINED, PROTECTIVE.

LIKES: ROAMING OPEN PLAINS, HELPING OTHERS, DISCOVERING HIDDEN PATHS.

DISLIKES: UNFAIRNESS, DANGER TO FRIENDS, BEING MISUNDERSTOOD.

FUN FACT: LESARA'S HORN CAN BREAK THROUGH THE TOUGHEST BARRIERS IN VARIANCE!

LESARA'S COURAGEOUS CLIMB

IN THE MAJESTIC LAND OF VARIANCE, WHERE MOUNTAINS REACHED FOR THE SKY, LESARA THE DETERMINED RHINO STOOD AS A SYMBOL OF UNWAVERING COURAGE. HIGH IN THE PEAKS, A LEGENDARY FLOWER KNOWN AS THE "SKY BLOSSOM" BLOOMED, SAID TO GRANT IMMENSE STRENGTH TO ANYONE WHO REACHED IT. INSPIRED BY TALES OF ITS POWER, LESARA EMBARKED ON A CHALLENGING CLIMB. THROUGH ROCKY TERRAIN AND SWIRLING MISTS, LESARA PRESSED ON, DRIVEN BY A DETERMINATION THAT COULD NOT BE SHAKEN. AS LESARA FINALLY BEHELD THE RADIANT SKY BLOSSOM, THE VERY AIR SEEMED TO HUM WITH ENERGY. WITH PETALS IN HAND, LESARA DESCENDED, EMBODYING THE TRUE STRENGTH THAT COMES FROM WITHIN.

Activity: Create a Magical Rhyme

Lesara loves to explore the land of Variance with her rhymes. Use your imagination to create a magical rhyme inspired by Lesara's adventures. Your rhyme could be about an enchanted forest, a hidden treasure, or a friendly encounter with a mythical creature.

Think of a magical theme for your rhyme. It could be about an adventure, friendship, or a special place.

- Write the first line of your rhyme on the lines provided.
- Use your creativity to come up with rhyming words for each line.

Example:

In the land of Variance so grand,
Where unicorns and fairies stand,
Adventure waits at every turn,
With lessons learned and stories to learn.

Remember, rhyming words have similar sounds!

Now it's your turn to create a magical rhyme !

_____

_____

_____

_____

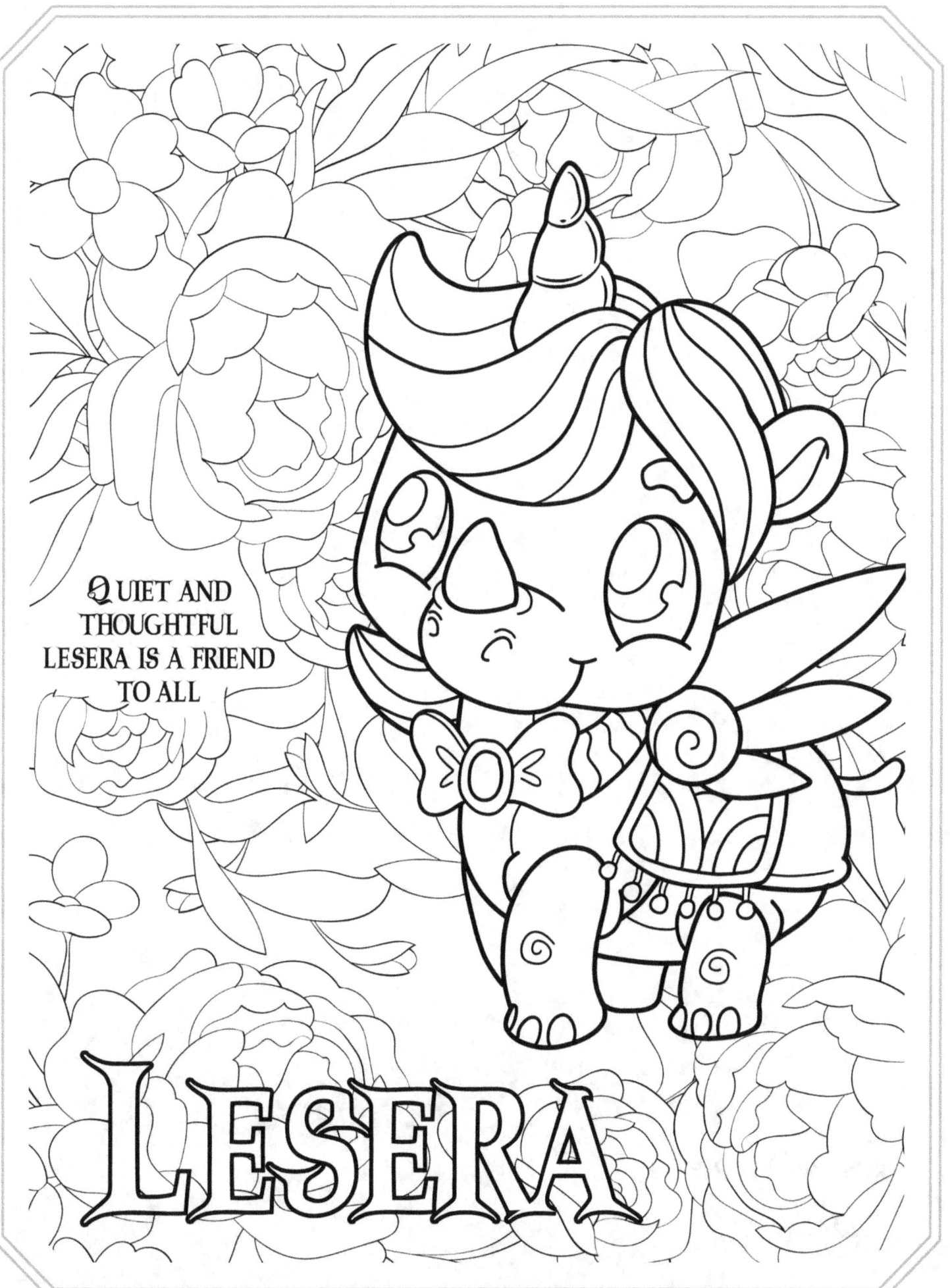

QUIET AND
THOUGHTFUL
LESERA IS A FRIEND
TO ALL

LESERA

Completed By:

Date:

SWARTHY

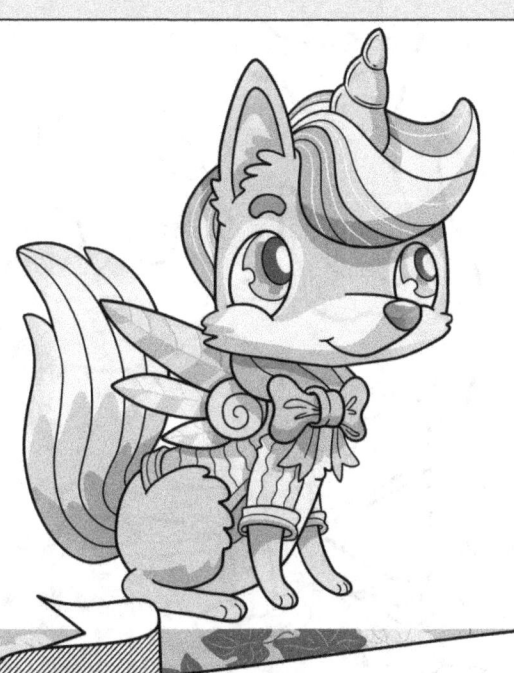

TRAITS: CLEVER, CUNNING, ADAPTABLE.

LIKES: SOLVING PUZZLES, OUTSMARTING CHALLENGES, DISCOVERING HIDDEN PATHS.

DISLIKES: BEING FOOLED, UNFAIR SITUATIONS, BEING UNDERESTIMATED.

FUN FACT: SWARTHY HAS A SECRET MAP THAT LEADS TO THE MOST DELICIOUS BERRY BUSHES!

SWARTHY'S WHIMSICAL WONDERS

IN THE ENCHANTING LAND OF VARIANCE, WHERE IMAGINATION PAINTED THE SKIES, SWARTHY THE MISCHIEVOUS FOX WAS A MASTER OF WHIMSY. WITH A TWINKLE IN HIS EYE AND A MISCHIEVOUS GRIN, SWARTHY BROUGHT LAUGHTER AND JOY TO EVERY CORNER OF VARIANCE. ONE DAY, SWARTHY STUMBLED UPON A FORGOTTEN GARDEN, OVERGROWN WITH MAGICAL PLANTS. AS SWARTHY EXPLORED, THE PLANTS SEEMED TO COME ALIVE, PAINTING THE GARDEN WITH VIVID COLORS AND ENCHANTING MELODIES. SWARTHY'S LAUGHTER JOINED THE SYMPHONY, AND THE GARDEN'S MAGIC SWIRLED AROUND HIM. FROM THAT DAY ON, SWARTHY BECAME THE KEEPER OF WHIMSY, SHARING THE MAGIC OF THE GARDEN WITH ALL WHO CROSSED HIS PATH.

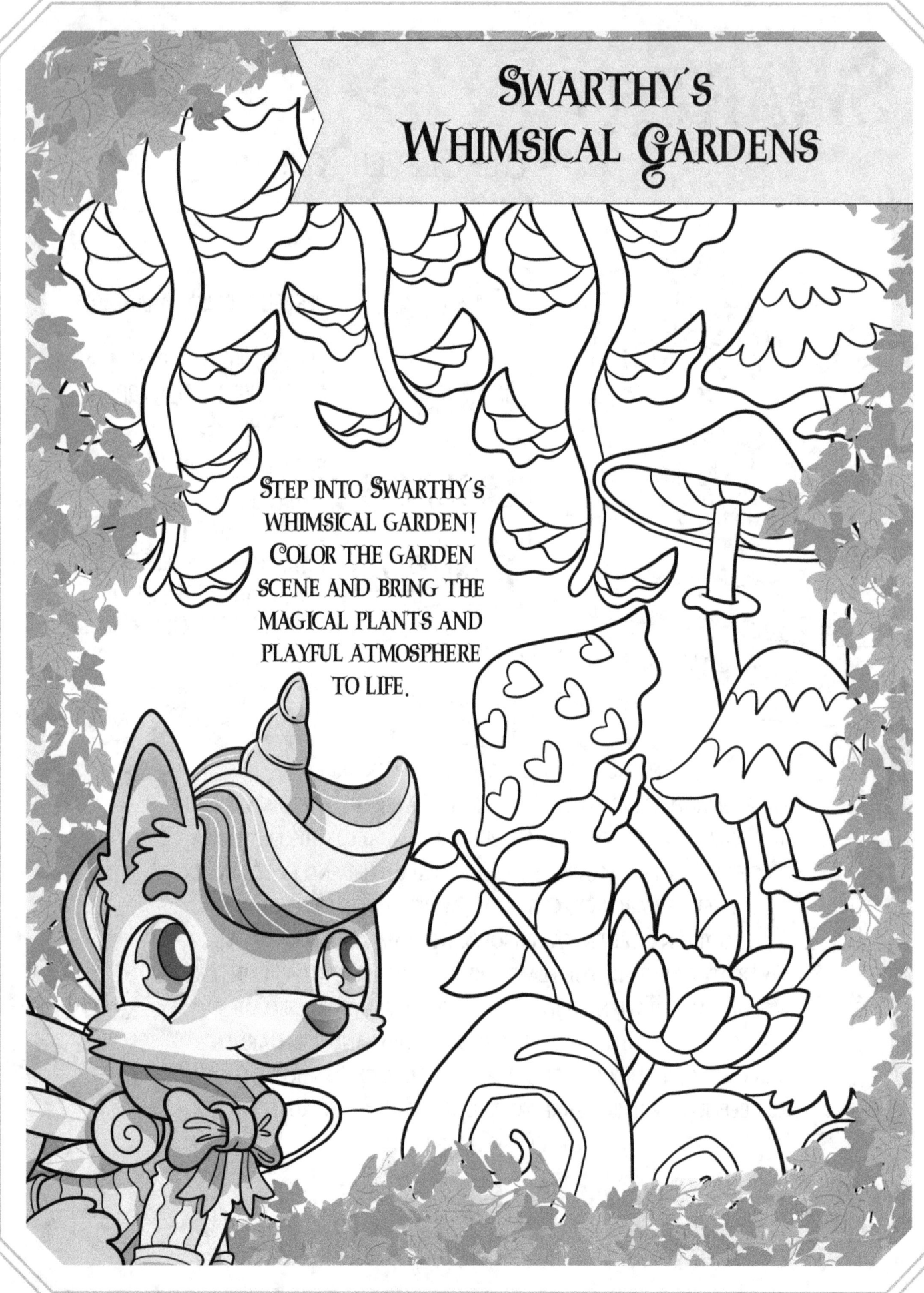

Swarthy's Whimsical Gardens

Step into Swarthy's whimsical garden! Color the garden scene and bring the magical plants and playful atmosphere to life.

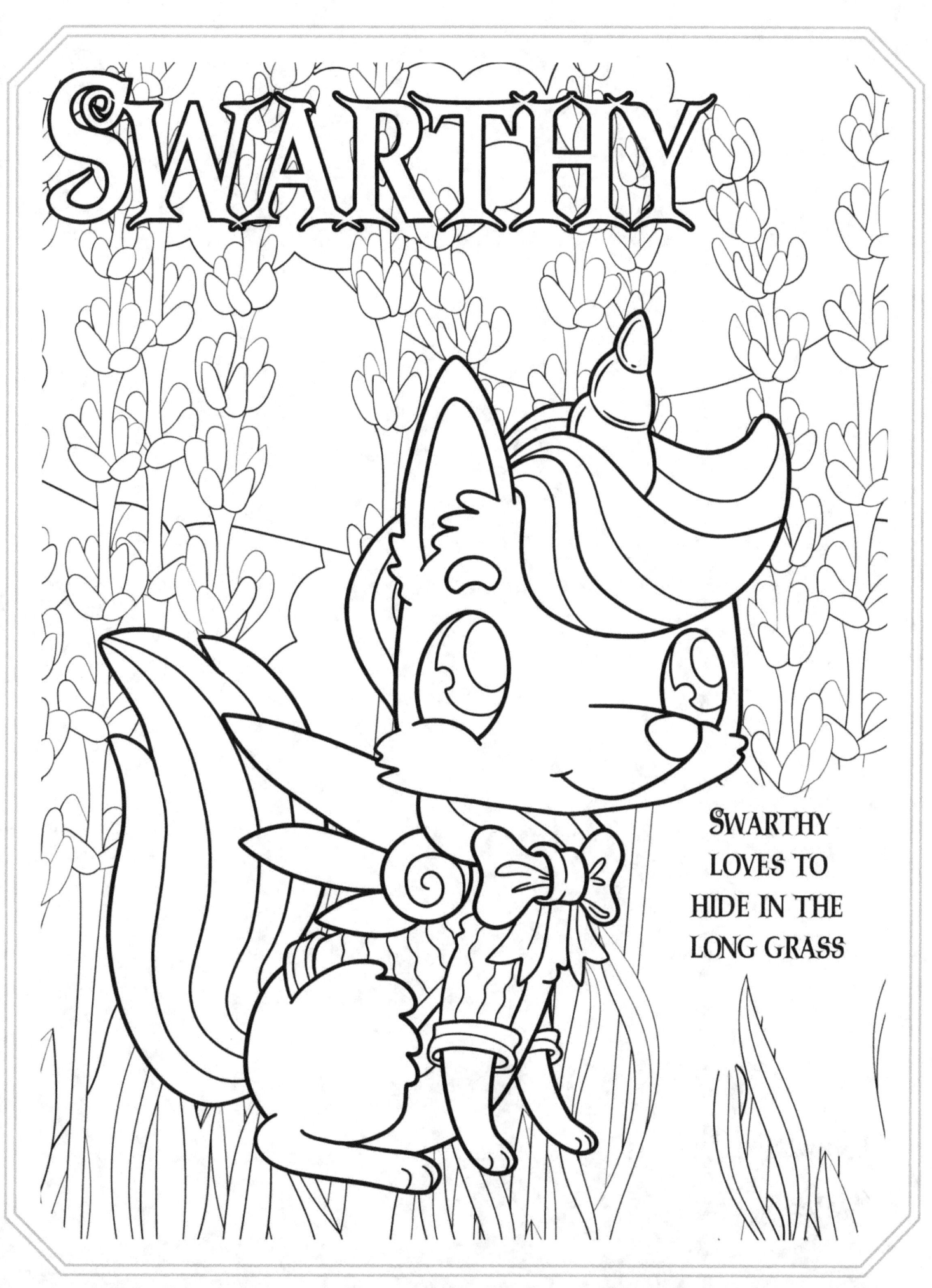

Completed By:

Date:

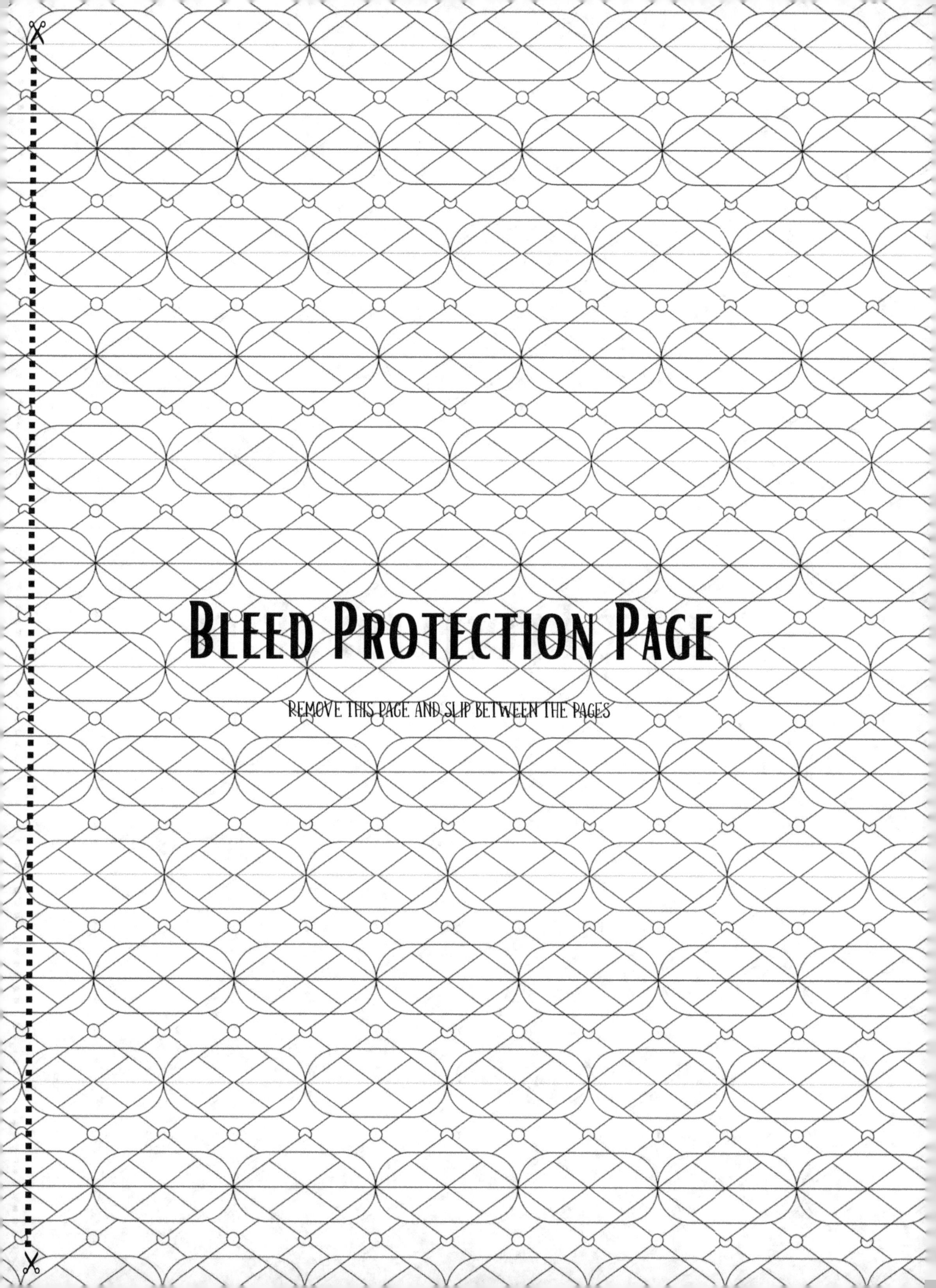

BLEED PROTECTION PAGE

REMOVE THIS PAGE AND SLIP BETWEEN THE PAGES

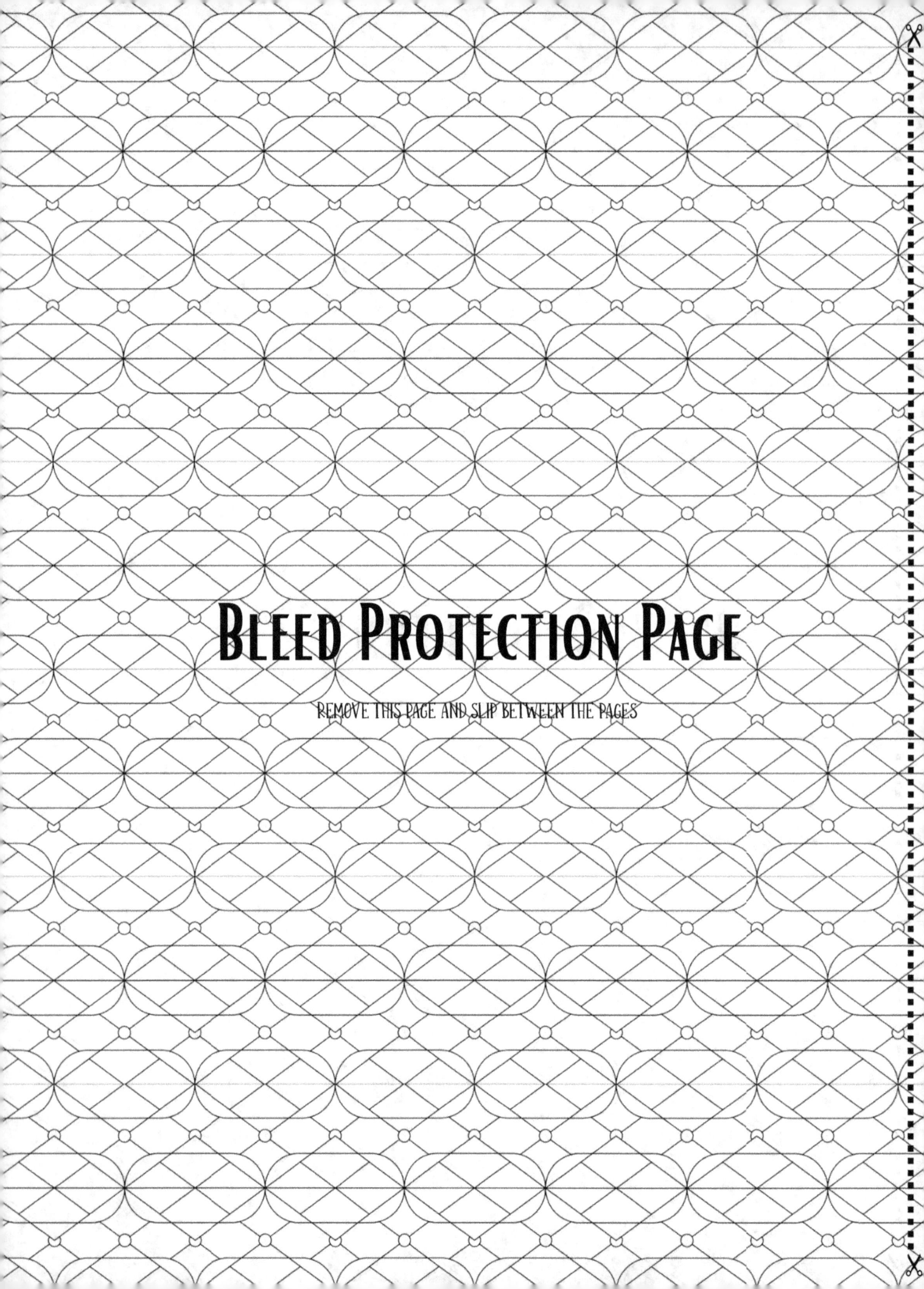

Bleed Protection Page

REMOVE THIS PAGE AND SLIP BETWEEN THE PAGES

Follow Us On Amazon

TKTCollection Publishing

SCAN HERE

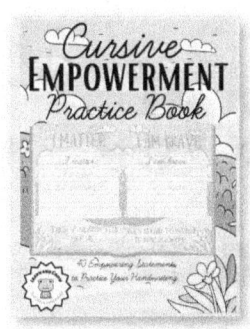

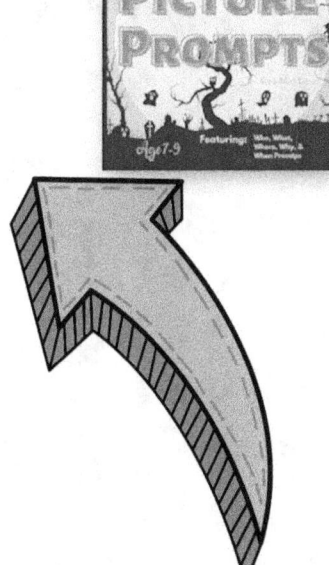

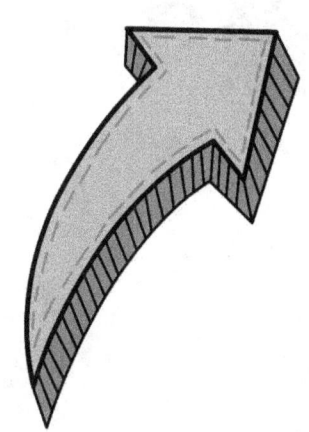

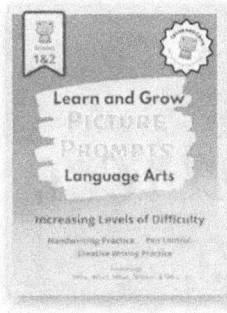

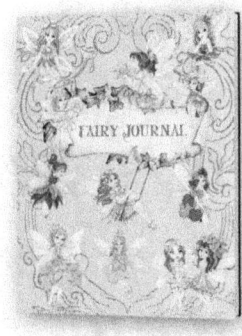

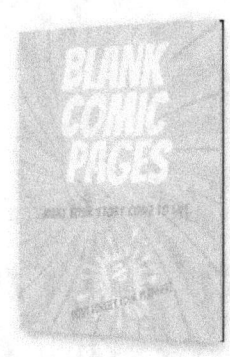

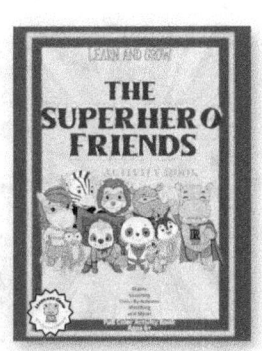

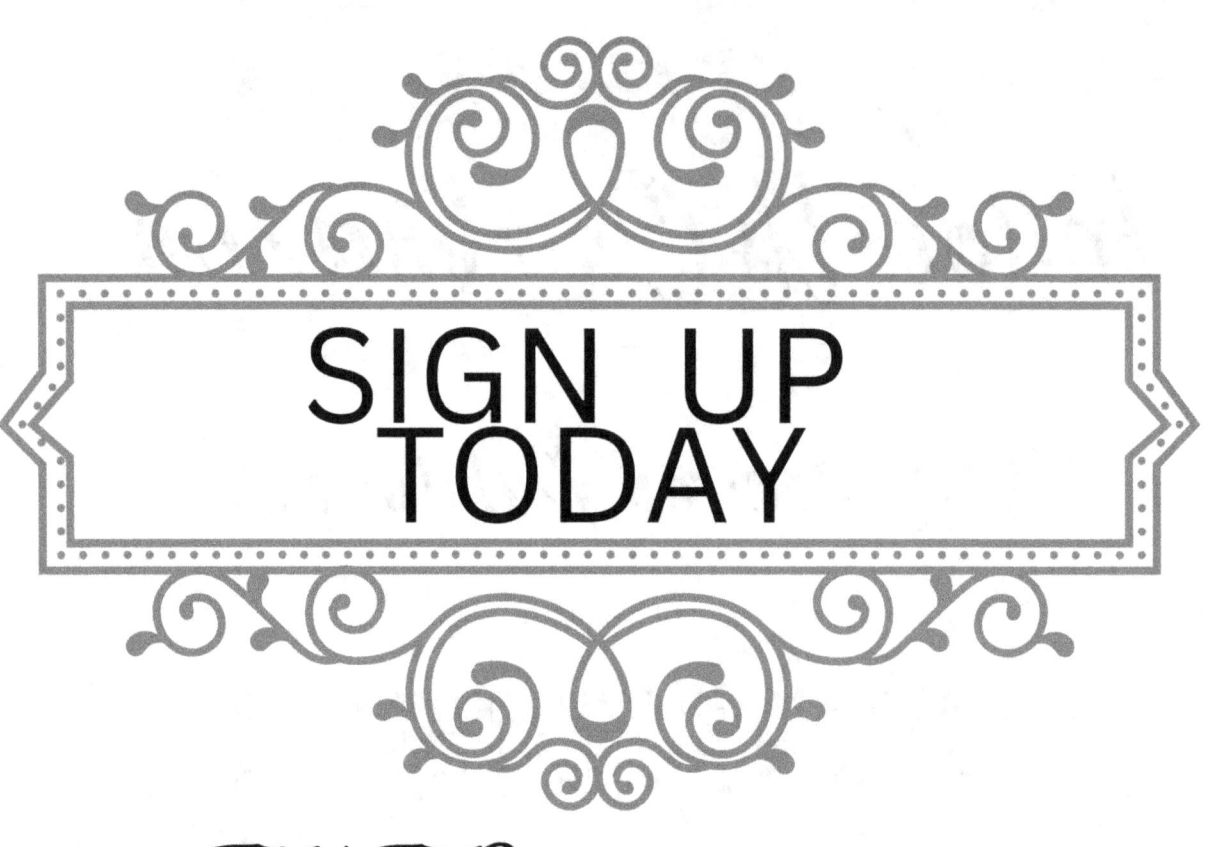

SIGN UP TODAY

TKTCollection

Newsletter

New Releases, In Person Appearances, Special Offers and Freebies. Sign Up Today!